THE HISTORY OF MANCHESTER UNITED IN COMIC STRIP

MAN UTD

THE GRAPHIC STORY

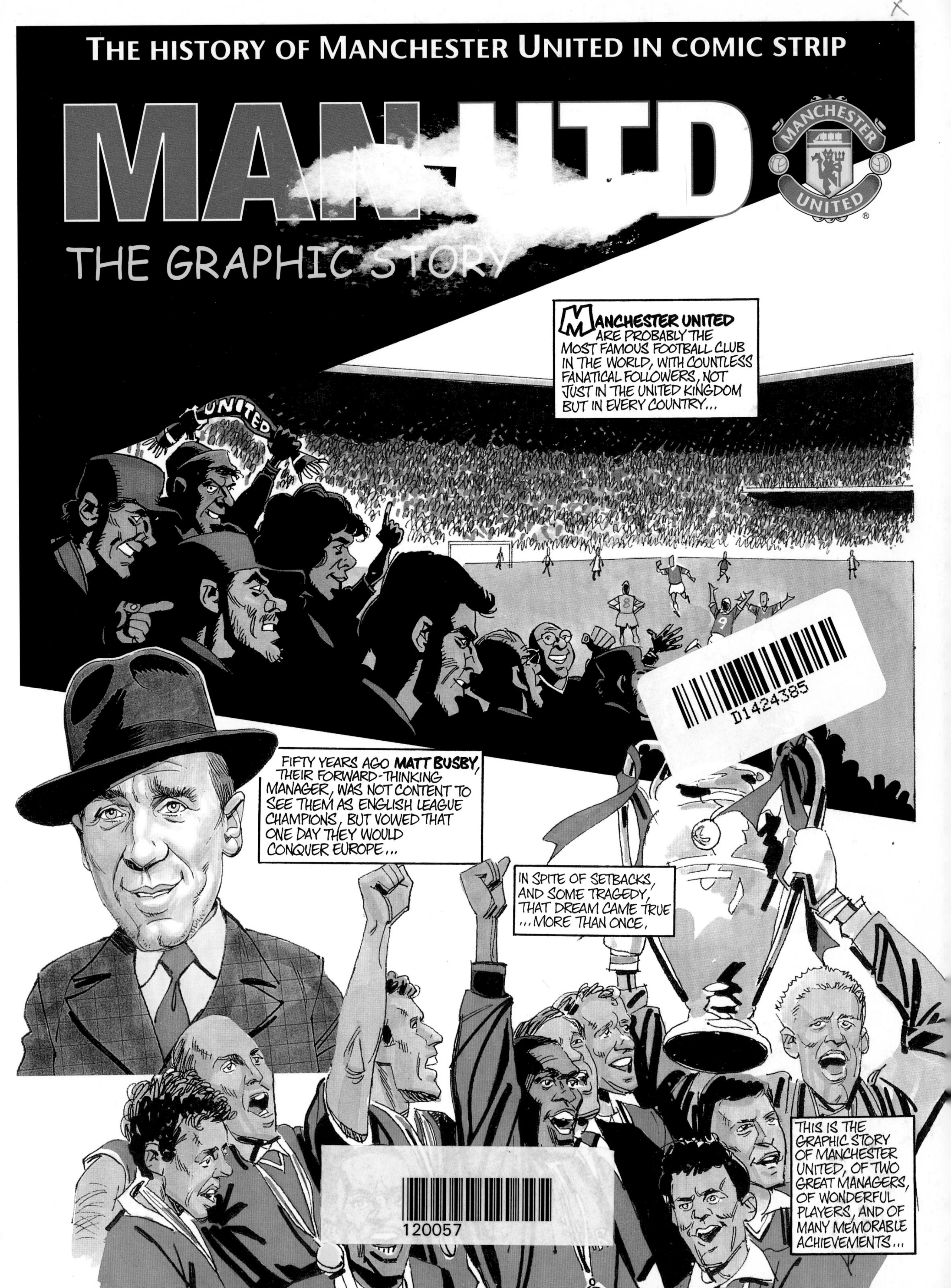
MANCHESTER UNITED ARE PROBABLY THE MOST FAMOUS FOOTBALL CLUB IN THE WORLD, WITH COUNTLESS FANATICAL FOLLOWERS, NOT JUST IN THE UNITED KINGDOM BUT IN EVERY COUNTRY...
FIFTY YEARS AGO MATT BUSBY, THEIR FORWARD-THINKING MANAGER, WAS NOT CONTENT TO SEE THEM AS ENGLISH LEAGUE CHAMPIONS, BUT VOWED THAT ONE DAY THEY WOULD CONQUER EUROPE...
IN SPITE OF SETBACKS, AND SOME TRAGEDY, THAT DREAM CAME TRUE ...MORE THAN ONCE.
THIS IS THE GRAPHIC STORY OF MANCHESTER UNITED, OF TWO GREAT MANAGERS, OF WONDERFUL PLAYERS, AND OF MANY MEMORABLE ACHIEVEMENTS...

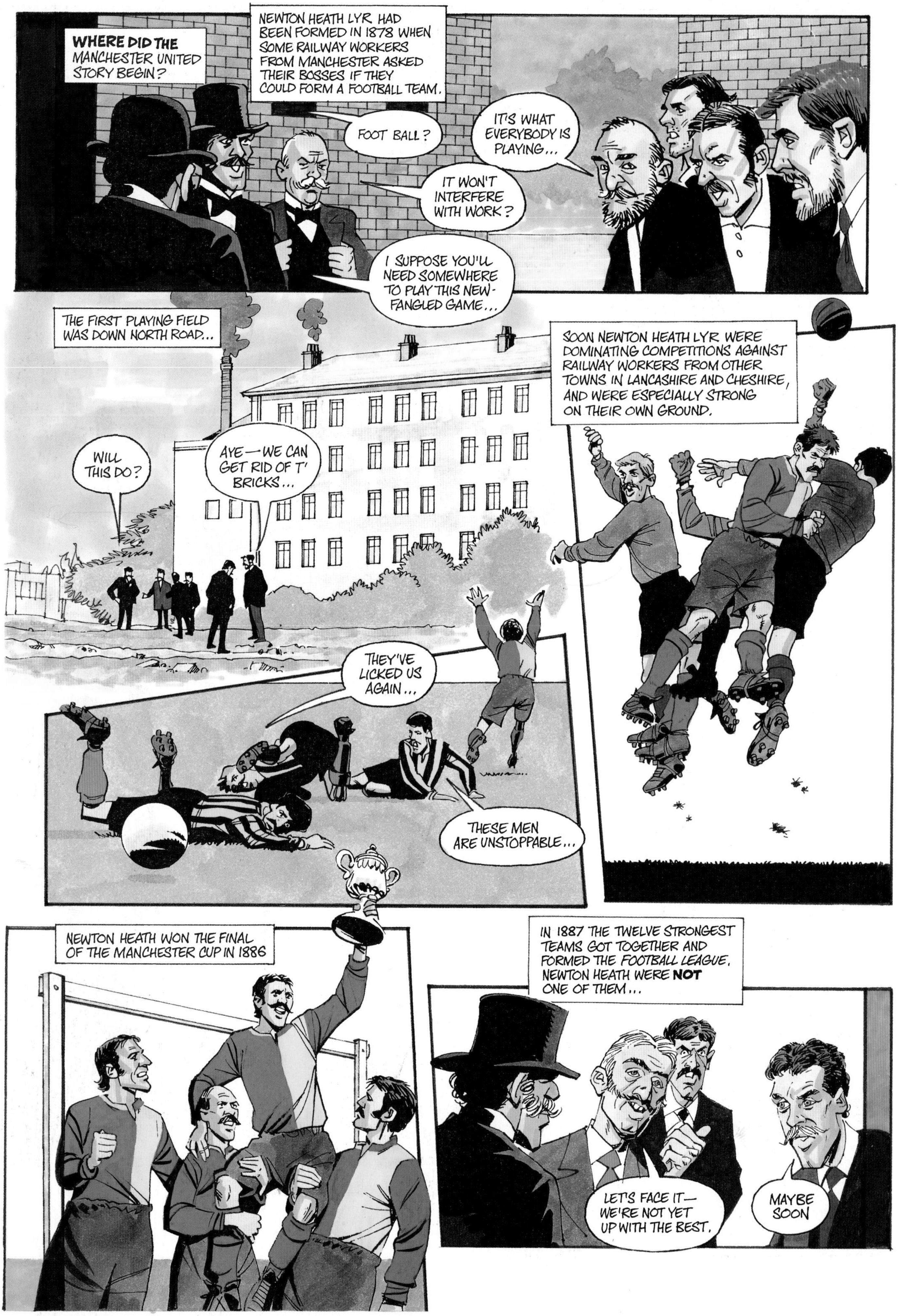
WHERE DID THE MANCHESTER UNITED STORY BEGIN?
NEWTON HEATH LYR HAD BEEN FORMED IN 1878 WHEN SOME RAILWAY WORKERS FROM MANCHESTER ASKED THEIR BOSSES IF THEY COULD FORM A FOOTBALL TEAM.
FOOT BALL?
IT'S WHAT EVERYBODY IS PLAYING...
IT WON'T INTERFERE WITH WORK?
I SUPPOSE YOU'LL NEED SOMEWHERE TO PLAY THIS NEW-FANGLED GAME...
THE FIRST PLAYING FIELD WAS DOWN NORTH ROAD...
WILL THIS DO?
AYE—WE CAN GET RID OF T' BRICKS...
SOON NEWTON HEATH LYR WERE DOMINATING COMPETITIONS AGAINST RAILWAY WORKERS FROM OTHER TOWNS IN LANCASHIRE AND CHESHIRE, AND WERE ESPECIALLY STRONG ON THEIR OWN GROUND.
THEY'VE LICKED US AGAIN...
THESE MEN ARE UNSTOPPABLE...
NEWTON HEATH WON THE FINAL OF THE MANCHESTER CUP IN 1886
IN 1887 THE TWELVE STRONGEST TEAMS GOT TOGETHER AND FORMED THE FOOTBALL LEAGUE. NEWTON HEATH WERE NOT ONE OF THEM...
LET'S FACE IT—WE'RE NOT YET UP WITH THE BEST.
MAYBE SOON

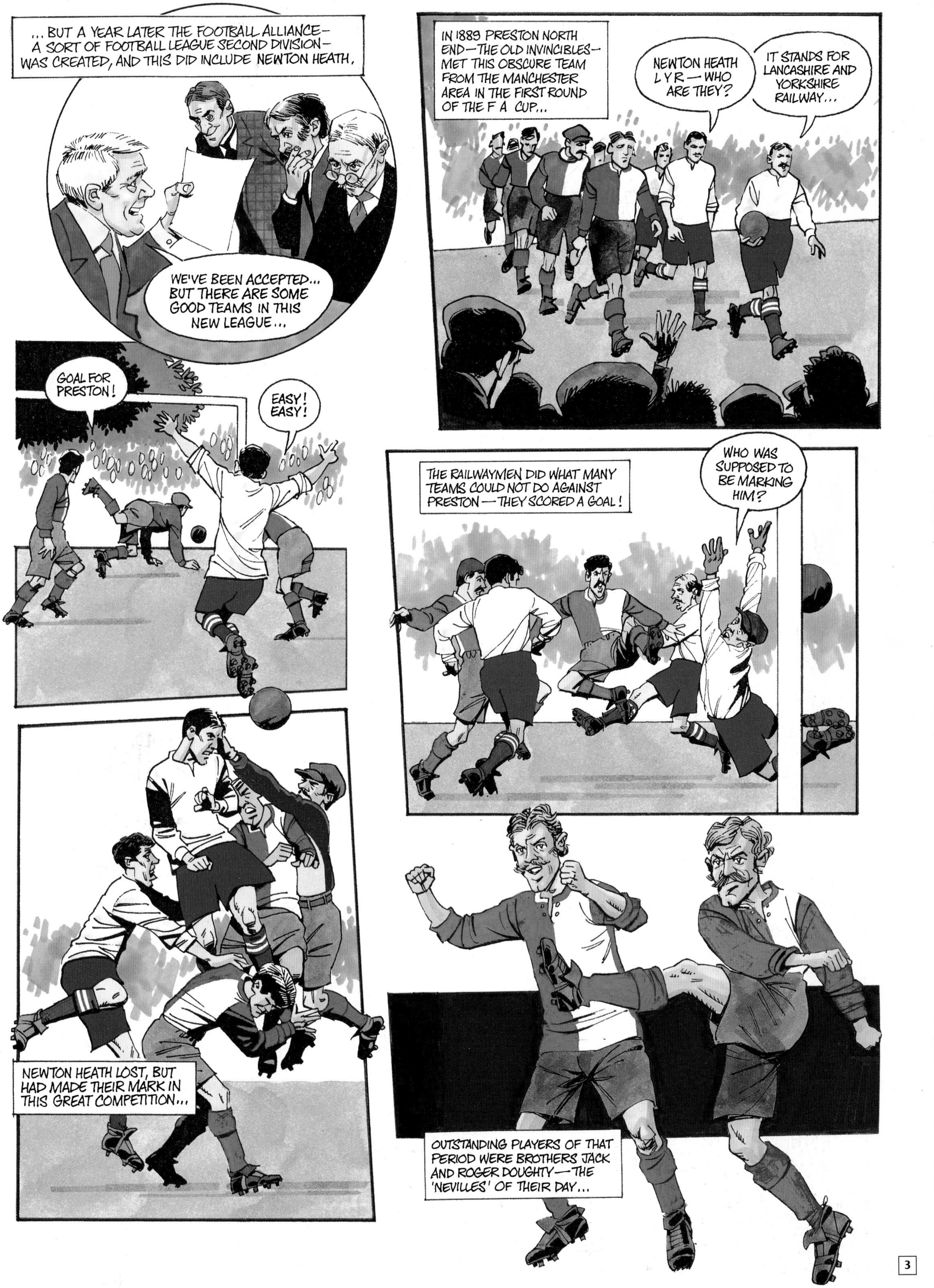

... BUT A YEAR LATER THE FOOTBALL ALLIANCE– A SORT OF FOOTBALL LEAGUE SECOND DIVISION– WAS CREATED, AND THIS DID INCLUDE NEWTON HEATH.
WE'VE BEEN ACCEPTED... BUT THERE ARE SOME GOOD TEAMS IN THIS NEW LEAGUE...
IN 1889 PRESTON NORTH END–THE OLD INVINCIBLES– MET THIS OBSCURE TEAM FROM THE MANCHESTER AREA IN THE FIRST ROUND OF THE F A CUP...
NEWTON HEATH L Y R — WHO ARE THEY?
IT STANDS FOR LANCASHIRE AND YORKSHIRE RAILWAY...
GOAL FOR PRESTON!
EASY! EASY!
THE RAILWAYMEN DID WHAT MANY TEAMS COULD NOT DO AGAINST PRESTON — THEY SCORED A GOAL!
WHO WAS SUPPOSED TO BE MARKING HIM?
NEWTON HEATH LOST, BUT HAD MADE THEIR MARK IN THIS GREAT COMPETITION...
OUTSTANDING PLAYERS OF THAT PERIOD WERE BROTHERS JACK AND ROGER DOUGHTY — THE 'NEVILLES' OF THEIR DAY...

THE FOOTBALL ALLIANCE ALSO INCLUDED A TEAM CALLED ARDWICK, WHO PLAYED NEWTON HEATH FOR THE FIRST TIME ON THE IMPREGNABLE NORTH ROAD PITCH...

...A SIGNIFICANT MEETING, BECAUSE NEWTON HEATH WOULD LATER BECOME MANCHESTER UNITED, AND ARDWICK CHANGED THEIR NAME TO MANCHESTER CITY...

IN 1892 NEWTON HEATH JOINED THE ELITE OF THE FIRST DIVISION, AND A YEAR LATER MOVED TO A NEW GROUND AT CLAYTON.

SMILE PLEASE INSIDE-LEFT... AND WATCH THE BIRDIE!

BUT SUCCESS AT THE VERY TOP DID NOT COME STRAIGHT AWAY. THEY COULD NOT COMPETE EASILY WITH TEAMS LIKE ASTON VILLA, EVERTON AND PRESTON.

COME ON, HEATHENS! YOU'RE ONLY THREE DOWN...

BOO! RUBBISH!

BOOOO!

IN 1894 THEY WERE RELEGATED...

AFTER TEN VERY ORDINARY YEARS NEWTON HEATH WERE BACK IN DIVISION TWO, AND ON THE EDGE OF BANKRUPTCY WHEN CLUB CAPTAIN HARRY STAFFORD AND FOUR BUSINESSMEN STEPPED IN WITH A RESCUE PACKAGE...

WE MUST NO LONGER GO ON CALLING OURSELVES NEWTON HEATH.

WE NEED A NEW NAME...

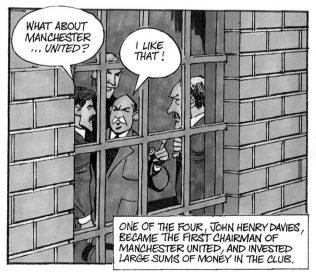

WHAT ABOUT MANCHESTER ...UNITED?

I LIKE THAT!

ONE OF THE FOUR, JOHN HENRY DAVIES, BECAME THE FIRST CHAIRMAN OF MANCHESTER UNITED, AND INVESTED LARGE SUMS OF MONEY IN THE CLUB.

IN 1906 MANCHESTER UNITED WON PROMOTION TO THE FIRST DIVISION — A FAMOUS NAME IN A FAMOUS LEAGUE FOR THE FIRST TIME.

MANCHESTER UNITED WON THE FIRST DIVISION TITLE FOR THE FIRST TIME IN 1908.

THE SAME YEAR MANCHESTER UNITED PLAYED ON THE CONTINENT FOR THE FIRST TIME... A SUMMER TOUR OF AUSTRIA AND HUNGARY. AFTER BEATING THE LOCAL FAVOURITES **7-0**, UNITED WERE ATTACKED WITH STICKS AND STONES BY THE DISGRUNTLED HUNGARIAN SPECTATORS... FOOTBALL HOOLIGANISM IN 1908!

WHAT'S GOING ON? IT'S ONLY A FOOTBALL MATCH...

BUDAPEST? NEVER AGAIN!

IT HAPPENED IN ENGLAND AS WELL — UNITED PLAYERS WERE PELTED WITH MUD AND STONES AT BRADFORD.

CHARLIE ROBERTS WAS A MAGNIFICENT CENTRE-HALF, BOUGHT FROM GRIMSBY FOR A STAGGERING £600! HE ALSO CREATED A SENSATION BY WEARING VERY SHORT SHORTS...

BUT CHARLIE, YOU CAN'T GO OUT THERE LIKE **THAT**... IT'S NOT DECENT!

ANOTHER IMPORTANT CAPTURE WAS BILLY MEREDITH, A FREE TRANSFER FROM MANCHESTER CITY, BUT COSTING A £500 SIGNING-ON FEE GOING TO THE PLAYER HIMSELF, ONE OF SOCCER'S IMMORTALS, MEREDITH WON 48 CAPS FOR WALES, AND WAS STILL PLAYING AT THE AGE OF 51...

IN MARCH 1909 AN F A CUP TIE AT BURNLEY WAS ABANDONED BECAUSE OF A BLINDING SNOWSTORM WITH UNITED TRAILING 0-1...

AW, REF, WE CAN'T SEE A THING...

NOT ONLY DID UNITED WIN THE REPLAYED GAME, BUT THEY GOT THROUGH TO THE CUP FINAL ITSELF FOR THE FIRST TIME.

BRISTOL CITY WERE UNITED'S OPPONENTS IN THE FINAL AT CRYSTAL PALACE, AND MANY TRAINS CARRIED THOUSANDS OF SUPPORTERS TO THE CAPITAL FROM THE NORTH AND WEST...

COME ON, UNITED!

SANDY TURNBULL SCORED THE ONLY GOAL OF THE MATCH FOR UNITED. MEREDITH WAS THE BEST PLAYER AFIELD, BRINGING HOME A SECOND WINNER'S MEDAL TO ADD TO THE ONE HE WON WITH CITY IN 1904.

WHEN SKIPPER CHARLIE ROBERTS AND HIS VICTORIOUS TEAM RETURNED TO MANCHESTER WITH THE SILVER CUP, THOUSANDS OF HAPPY FANS LINED THE ROUTE.

A YEAR LATER UNITED MOVED AGAIN — TO A THIRD NEW GROUND AT OLD TRAFFORD.

IT WAS TO HOLD A RECORD 76,962 SPECTATORS FOR A MATCH IN 1939, BEFORE BECOMING THE *THEATRE OF DREAMS* THAT IT IS TODAY.

IN 1911, ON THE LAST SATURDAY OF THE SEASON, VILLA LED THE FIRST DIVISION BY A SINGLE POINT FROM UNITED, WHO WERE AT HOME TO SUNDERLAND...

JUST GO OUT THERE AND WIN, AND FORGET WHAT VILLA ARE DOING.

GOAL— OH, YOU BEAUTY!

WIN UNITED DID, BY 5-1...

...AND ON RETURNING TO THE DRESSING ROOM WERE GIVEN THE BEST POSSIBLE NEWS.

VILLA HAVE **LOST**! WELL DONE, LADS—YOU'RE THE CHAMPIONS!

TWO WORLD WARS WOULD INTERVENE BEFORE UNITED'S NEXT MAJOR HONOUR...

BRITO

YOU

THEY SPENT MANY HARD YEARS IN DIVISION TWO, AND WERE WITHIN A WHISKER OF DIVISION THREE...

FOR THE FINAL MATCH OF THE 1933-34 SEASON THEY VISITED MILLWALL, KNOWING THAT ONLY A WIN WOULD SAVE THEM...

NO...

YES!

A 2-0 VICTORY KEPT UNITED UP, AND SENT MILLWALL DOWN TO DIVISION THREE INSTEAD.

MATT BUSBY HAD ENDED A SUCCESSFUL PLAYING CAREER WITH MANCHESTER CITY AND LIVERPOOL WHEN HE WAS APPOINTED MANAGER OF MANCHESTER UNITED IN 1945, THE NEW BOSS LOOKED OUT OVER A BOMBED OLD TRAFFORD...

WELL, HERE I AM... A DERELICT GROUND... NO MONEY... WHAT A MESS! I'M GOING TO NEED MORE STRENGTH THAN I HAVE...

BUT UNITED WERE BACK IN THE FIRST DIVISION, AND HAD NEARLY ALL THE PLAYERS THEY NEEDED TO SUCCEED.

JACK ROWLEY CENTRE-FORWARD

JOHNNY CAREY FULL-BACK

CAREY AND ROWLEY WERE JUST TWO OF A STAR-STUDDED SIDE, PACKED WITH FUTURE INTERNATIONALS.

ONLY WINGER JIMMY DELANEY, A £4,000 SIGNING FROM CELTIC, WAS ADDED TO THE SQUAD, AND UNITED FINISHED SECOND IN DIVISION ONE IN 1947-48.

THE BOSS GETS UP HIGHER THAN ANY OF US...

THE OLD-STYLE MANAGER WORE A SUIT AND SPATS AND SAT AT A DESK, BUT MATT BUSBY WAS ONE OF THE FIRST TRACK-SUITED MANAGERS, GETTING OUT THERE AND COACHING AND WORKING WITH HIS PLAYERS.

WHILE OLD TRAFFORD WAS BEING REBUILT, UNITED HAD TO PLAY THEIR HOME GAMES AT MAINE ROAD, MANCHESTER CITY'S GROUND...

THE SAME SEASON IN THE F A CUP THEY WON AN ABSOLUTE THRILLER AT VILLA PARK, 5-1 UP AT HALF-TIME, UNITED REELED AND ROCKED AS ASTON VILLA FOUGHT BACK TO 5-4... THEN CLINCHED THE GAME WITH A LATE SIXTH GOAL...

BRILLIANT!

HOW MANY IS THAT?

I'VE LOST COUNT...

ARE WE STILL WINNING?

WHAT A GAME!

IT WAS THE FIRST STEP ON THE WAY TO WEMBLEY, AND AN F A CUP FINAL AGAINST BLACKPOOL.

THIS, TOO, WAS A THRILL-PACKED GAME...

COME ON BLACKPOOL!

MATTHEWS HAS THE BALL...

BLACKPOOL, WITH THE FAMOUS STANLEY MATTHEWS, LED TWICE.

BUT ENGLAND'S JACK ROWLEY EQUALISED BOTH TIMES...

IT'S IN THE NET!

THEN THE DECISIVE FEW SECONDS...

OOO

OH!

UNITED GOALKEEPER JACK CROMPTON SAVED BRILLIANTLY FROM STAN MORTENSEN...

...A QUICK CLEARANCE...

PICK THAT ONE OUT!

...AND BEFORE THE CHEERING STOPPED STAN PEARSON HAD THE BALL IN THE BLACKPOOL NET AT THE OTHER END.

MANCHESTER UNITED WENT ON TO WIN 4-2 WITH JOHNNY CAREY, A TOUGH BUT GENIAL SKIPPER, LIFTING THE CUP.

UNITED!

WELL PLAYED UNITED!

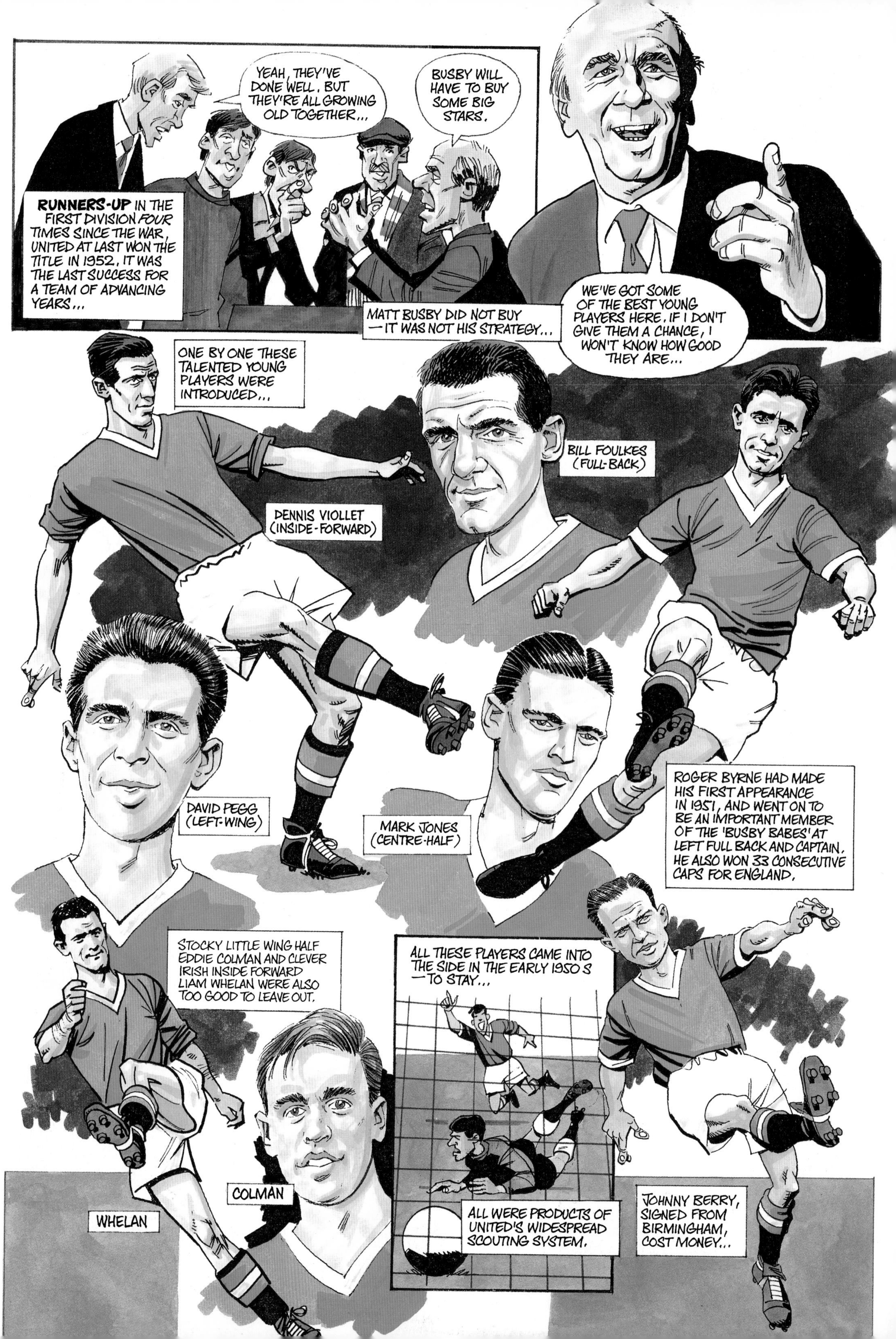
YEAH, THEY'VE DONE WELL. BUT THEY'RE ALL GROWING OLD TOGETHER...
BUSBY WILL HAVE TO BUY SOME BIG STARS.
RUNNERS-UP IN THE FIRST DIVISION FOUR TIMES SINCE THE WAR, UNITED AT LAST WON THE TITLE IN 1952. IT WAS THE LAST SUCCESS FOR A TEAM OF ADVANCING YEARS...
MATT BUSBY DID NOT BUY —IT WAS NOT HIS STRATEGY...
WE'VE GOT SOME OF THE BEST YOUNG PLAYERS HERE. IF I DON'T GIVE THEM A CHANCE, I WON'T KNOW HOW GOOD THEY ARE...
ONE BY ONE THESE TALENTED YOUNG PLAYERS WERE INTRODUCED...
BILL FOULKES (FULL-BACK)
DENNIS VIOLLET (INSIDE-FORWARD)
DAVID PEGG (LEFT-WING)
MARK JONES (CENTRE-HALF)
ROGER BYRNE HAD MADE HIS FIRST APPEARANCE IN 1951, AND WENT ON TO BE AN IMPORTANT MEMBER OF THE 'BUSBY BABES' AT LEFT FULL BACK AND CAPTAIN. HE ALSO WON 33 CONSECUTIVE CAPS FOR ENGLAND.
STOCKY LITTLE WING HALF EDDIE COLMAN AND CLEVER IRISH INSIDE FORWARD LIAM WHELAN WERE ALSO TOO GOOD TO LEAVE OUT.
ALL THESE PLAYERS CAME INTO THE SIDE IN THE EARLY 1950 S —TO STAY...
COLMAN
WHELAN
ALL WERE PRODUCTS OF UNITED'S WIDESPREAD SCOUTING SYSTEM.
JOHNNY BERRY, SIGNED FROM BIRMINGHAM, COST MONEY...

SO DID TOMMY TAYLOR, WHO WAS BOUGHT FROM BARNSLEY IN 1953. HE DIDN'T WANT TO BE LUMBERED WITH A £30,000 FEE, SO THE PRICE WAS AGREED AT £29,999!

TAYLOR SOON PROVED TO BE WORTH EVERY PENNY, AND HE TOO BECAME AN ENGLAND REGULAR.

DUNCAN EDWARDS MAY HAVE BEEN THE GREATEST OF THEM ALL.

BORN IN DUDLEY, HE SIGNED AMATEUR FORMS FOR UNITED AS A SCHOOLBOY IN 1952, AND MADE HIS FIRST DIVISION DEBUT AT 16...

HE WAS THE YOUNGEST PLAYER TO PLAY FOR ENGLAND UNTIL MICHAEL OWEN IN THE 1990'S...

NEARLY 6 FEET TALL AND 13 STONE, EDWARDS HAD A SUPERB PHYSIQUE, AND DOMINATED THE MIDFIELD. HE COULD BURST THROUGH DEFENCES AND SCORE WITH AN EXPLOSIVE SHOT.

WHEN UNITED SWEPT TO THE FIRST DIVISION TITLE AGAIN IN 1955-56, ALL OF THESE YOUNG MEN HAD BECOME ESTABLISHED FIRST TEAM STARS. OPPONENTS WERE OVERCOME BY GREATER SKILL AND FITNESS...

11

A HARD-SHOOTING TEENAGER WAS ALSO KNOCKING ON THE DOOR. BOBBY CHARLTON MADE HIS FIRST DIVISION DEBUT IN OCTOBER 1956 AGAINST CHARLTON ATHLETIC, AND SCORED TWO BLISTERING GOALS...

IN 14 LEAGUE APPEARANCES THAT SEASON CHARLTON NETTED TEN TIMES.

MANCHESTER UNITED RACED TO ANOTHER TITLE, THEIR YOUNG SIDE SIMPLY GETTING BETTER EVERY WEEK. OVER 100 GOALS WERE SCORED...

...EXCEPT ASTON VILLA.

BUT UNITED LOST THEIR GOALKEEPER RAY WOOD FOLLOWING A COLLISION WITH A VILLA FORWARD...

THE REDS ALSO REACHED THE FA CUP FINAL, AND IT SEEMED NOTHING COULD STOP THEM BECOMING THE FIRST TEAM TO DO THE DOUBLE SINCE ASTON VILLA IN 1897...

NO SUBSTITUTES WERE ALLOWED THEN, AND THE HANDICAP PROVED TOO GREAT EVEN FOR UNITED. VILLA WON 2-1...

UNI-TED!

VILLA!

FOR THE FIRST TIME AN ENGLISH SIDE APPEARED IN THE EUROPEAN CUP...

UNITED SCORE TEN! ANDERLECHT NO ANSWER

AFTER AN EASY PASSAGE THROUGH THE PRELIMINARY ROUND, UNITED THEN BEAT BORUSSIA DORTMUND...

...THEN MET ATHLETIC BILBAO IN ONE OF THE MOST THRILLING EUROPEAN ENCOUNTERS.

IN THE FIRST LEG IN BILBAO THE SPANIARDS BUILT A 5-2 LEAD BEFORE, RIGHT ON THE FINAL WHISTLE, WHELAN SCORED A SUPERB GOAL. IT COULDN'T MAKE ANY DIFFERENCE, SURELY?

IN THE RETURN MATCH PLAYED AT MAINE ROAD, UNITED PULLED BACK BILBAO'S 5-3 LEAD...

GOAL!

THAT'S 5-5!

TAYLOR HAS SCORED AGAIN!

WITH FIVE MINUTES TO GO ON A PULSATING EVENING JOHNNY BERRY SWEPT IN TAYLOR'S PASS...

WE'RE THROUGH!

DEFEAT BY REAL MADRID IN THE SEMI-FINAL ONLY SERVED TO STRENGTHEN MATT BUSBY'S RESOLVE TO SUCCEED IN EUROPE...

13

IN FEBRUARY 1958, RETURNING FROM A SUCCESSFUL EUROPEAN CUP MATCH AGAINST RED STAR BELGRADE, THE PLANE CARRYING UNITED'S BRILLIANT YOUNG TEAM CRASHED AT MUNICH AIRPORT. MARK JONES, TOMMY TAYLOR, ROGER BYRNE, GEOFF BENT, EDDIE COLMAN, LIAM WHELAN AND DAVID PEGG WERE KILLED, AND DUNCAN EDWARDS DIED LATER FROM HIS INJURIES. IN ALL 23 PEOPLE DIED IN THE CRASH BUT SOME PLAYERS SURVIVED, AS WELL AS THEIR MANAGER MATT BUSBY, WHO BRAVELY REPEATED HIS DESIRE TO CONQUER EUROPE.

TWO WEEKS AFTER THE DISASTER MANCHESTER UNITED, PATCHED UP WITH RESERVES AND NEW SIGNINGS, BEAT SHEFFIELD WEDNESDAY 3-0 IN FRONT OF 60,000 TEARFUL FANS.

ON THAT SAME WAVE OF EMOTION UNITED WERE CARRIED THROUGH TO ANOTHER F A CUP FINAL.

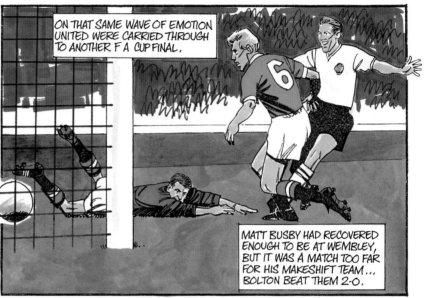

MATT BUSBY HAD RECOVERED ENOUGH TO BE AT WEMBLEY, BUT IT WAS A MATCH TOO FAR FOR HIS MAKESHIFT TEAM... BOLTON BEAT THEM 2-0.

IT WAS TO BE FIVE YEARS BEFORE UNITED REACHED WEMBLEY AGAIN...

BUSBY EMPTIED THE COFFERS TO BUY DENIS LAW FROM TORINO IN 1962, AND LAW SCORED THE FIRST GOAL IN THE FINAL OF 1963 AGAINST LEICESTER CITY.

UNITED HAD STRUGGLED IN THE LEAGUE BUT WON THE CUP 3-1. BILL FOULKES AND BOBBY CHARLTON WERE TWO OF THE SURVIVORS OF MUNICH, AND AFTER BEING LOSERS IN 1957 AND 1958, BOTH GAINED WINNERS' MEDALS AT LAST.

LAW WAS A SUPERB GOALSCORER. HE COULD SNIFF THE MEREST HALF-CHANCE. WHERE THAT CHANCE FELL, LAW WOULD BE THERE. IN 1963-64 HE SCORED 46 LEAGUE AND CUP GOALS IN 41 GAMES, INCLUDING SEVEN HAT-TRICKS.

A SKINNY IRISH LAD MADE HIS DEBUT THAT SEASON AND IMPRESSED EVERYONE WITH HIS CHEEKY SKILLS. HIS NAME WAS GEORGE BEST.

UNITED FINISHED SECOND TO LIVERPOOL IN 1964, BUT MADE NO MISTAKE THE FOLLOWING SEASON, SEVEN STRAIGHT WINS IN MARCH AND APRIL SEALED A SIXTH CHAMPIONSHIP.

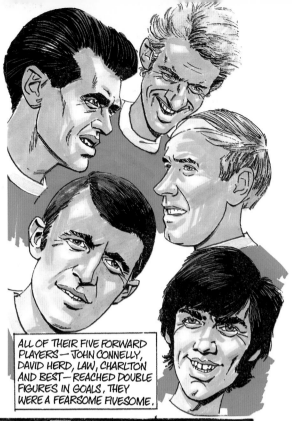

ALL OF THEIR FIVE FORWARD PLAYERS — JOHN CONNELLY, DAVID HERD, LAW, CHARLTON AND BEST — REACHED DOUBLE FIGURES IN GOALS, THEY WERE A FEARSOME FIVESOME.

MARCH 1966... ONE OF UNITED'S GREATEST PERFORMANCES, AGAINST BENFICA IN THE STADIUM OF LIGHT, IN THE EUROPEAN CUP...

...DEFENDING A SINGLE GOAL LEAD FROM THE FIRST LEG, UNITED WENT OUT AND SCORED *THREE* GOALS IN THE FIRST 15 MINUTES — TWO OF THEM FROM BEST.

WHEN CHARLTON WALTZED THROUGH TO SCORE UNITED'S FIFTH GOAL BENFICA HAD BEEN TORN APART—ON THEIR OWN GROUND!

THE PORTUGUESE PRESS CHRISTENED BEST 'EL BEATLE' AS HE CONTINUALLY CUT THROUGH THEIR DEFENCE.

SURPRISINGLY, THEY THEN LOST IN THE SEMI-FINAL TO PARTIZAN BELGRADE...

IN 1967 MANCHESTER UNITED WON THE CHAMPIONSHIP AGAIN ... AND EARNED ONE MORE SHOT AT THE EUROPEAN CUP ...

SO IN MAY 1968, THE OCCASION ALL THEIR FANS HAD LONGED FOR ...

THEIR OPPONENTS IN THE EUROPEAN CUP FINAL AT WEMBLEY WERE THE BRILLIANT PORTUGUESE CHAMPIONS BENFICA, WHO HAD IN EUSEBIO ONE OF THE WORLD'S OUTSTANDING PLAYERS.

GOAL! CHARLTON HAS DONE IT!

BUT EVEN AFTER UNITED OPENED THE SCORING IN THE SECOND HALF, VICTORY WAS BY NO MEANS CERTAIN.

UNITED'S DEFENCE CAME UNDER INTENSE PRESSURE ...

HOW LONG TO GO?

IT CAME AS NO REAL SURPRISE WHEN GRAÇA DROVE IN THE EQUALISER WITH TEN MINUTES TO GO ...

THAT'S IT ... WE CAN'T WIN NOW ...

WE CAN'T HOLD OUT MUCH LONGER ...

BENFICA LOOKED CERTAIN WINNERS AT THAT STAGE. EUSEBIO BURST THROUGH TO SHOOT FROM POINT BLANK RANGE ...

I CAN'T LOOK ...

BUT ALEX STEPNEY SAVED BRILLIANTLY, AND UNITED WERE STILL ALIVE ...

1-1 AT THE END OF NORMAL TIME, AND IT WAS THEN THAT MATT BUSBY CALLED FOR ONE LAST SUPREME EFFORT ...

COME ON ... THEY'RE EVEN MORE TIRED THAN YOU ARE ...

IN SEVEN MINUTES BENFICA WERE DESTROYED BY A MEMORABLE TREBLE.

1 GEORGE BEST RAN ON TO STEPNEY'S LONG KICK, ROUNDED THE KEEPER AND SLID THE BALL HOME...

GOAL!

2 BRIAN KIDD, ON HIS 19TH. BIRTHDAY, HEADED ANOTHER...

GOAL!

GOAL!

3 AND BOBBY CHARLTON SHOT HIS SECOND OF THE NIGHT FROM KIDD'S PASS—4-1!

THE REFEREE'S WHISTLE SIGNALLED THE END, AND THE CELEBRATIONS BEGAN.

CHAMPIONS OF EUROPE!

UNITED!

BOYS...YOU'VE MADE ME SO PROUD!

CHARLTON HELD UP THE FAMOUS TROPHY, AND MATT BUSBY'S DREAM HAD BECOME A REALITY.

UNITED!

HEROES ALL—AND ONE HUGELY CONTENTED MANAGER...

THINGS DON'T GET ANY BETTER THAN THIS

UNITED, ENGLAND'S FIRST TEAM TO COMPETE IN THE EUROPEAN CUP, HAD BECOME THE FIRST ENGLISH TEAM TO WIN IT!

IN AN FA CUP TIE AT NORTHAMPTON IN 1970, GEORGE BEST SCORED SIX GOALS...

...BUT INDIVIDUAL PERFORMANCES APART, MANCHESTER UNITED'S EUROPEAN CUP WIN DID NOT HERALD A SUCCESSFUL DECADE FOR THE CLUB. MATT BUSBY RETIRED, TO BE SUCCEEDED BY WILF McGUINNESS, FRANK O'FARRELL AND TOMMY DOCHERTY.

CHARLTON PLAYED HIS LAST GAME FOR UNITED... AND LAW... AND BEST.

YEAR BY YEAR THEY SLIPPED FURTHER DOWN THE FIRST DIVISION, UNTIL IN APRIL 1974...

IF WE LOSE TODAY, WE'RE DOWN...

THE SECOND DIVISION— UNTHINKABLE!

WHO WERE UNITED'S OPPONENTS THAT DAY? NONE OTHER THAN MANCHESTER CITY, AT OLD TRAFFORD...

WITH MINUTES TO PLAY DENIS LAW, NOW A CITY PLAYER ONCE MORE, BACK-HEELED THE GOAL WHICH CONDEMNED UNITED TO THE SECOND DIVISION!

LAW SHOWED NO PLEASURE WHEN HIS GOAL WENT IN, BUT WALKED SOLEMNLY BACK TO THE CENTRE CIRCLE.

IT WAS A SAD, SAD DAY FOR UNITED.

BUT A YEAR LATER THEY WERE BACK, WITH THE IMMACULATE MARTIN BUCHAN LEADING THEM TO THE SECOND DIVISION TITLE.

BUCHAN WAS A BRILLIANT DEFENDER WHO USED THE BALL INTELLIGENTLY. HE WOULD HAVE GRACED ANY UNITED TEAM, PAST OR PRESENT. BOUGHT FROM ABERDEEN IN 1972, HE SPENT TWELVE SEASONS AT OLD TRAFFORD, MOSTLY AS CAPTAIN.

IN 1976 MANCHESTER UNITED GOT THROUGH TO THE CUP FINAL AGAIN. STEVE COPPELL AND GORDON HILL WERE SUPERB YOUNG WINGERS, AND HILL'S TWO GOALS SAW OFF DERBY IN THE SEMI-FINAL...

A SHOCK WAS IN STORE, HOWEVER, AT WEMBLEY...

OH, NO... SOUTHAMPTON HAVE SCORED...

THAT DEFEAT WAS A SETBACK, BUT UNITED RETURNED TO WEMBLEY THE FOLLOWING YEAR, WITH MUCH STIFFER OPPOSITION...

LIVERPOOL HAD ALREADY WON THE LEAGUE TITLE AND REACHED THE EUROPEAN CUP FINAL, AND WERE CERTAINLY FAVOURITES...

THREE GOALS IN FIVE MINUTES BROUGHT THE GAME TO LIFE...

PEARSON HAS GIVEN UNITED THE LEAD!

LIVERPOOL EQUALISED ALMOST IMMEDIATELY...

BUT UNITED GOT THE WINNER WHEN JIMMY GREENHOFF DEFLECTED A SHOT FROM LOU MACARI INTO THE NET!

A MONTH LATER MANAGER TOMMY DOCHERTY WAS SACKED... AND WAS SUCCEEDED BY DAVE SEXTON.

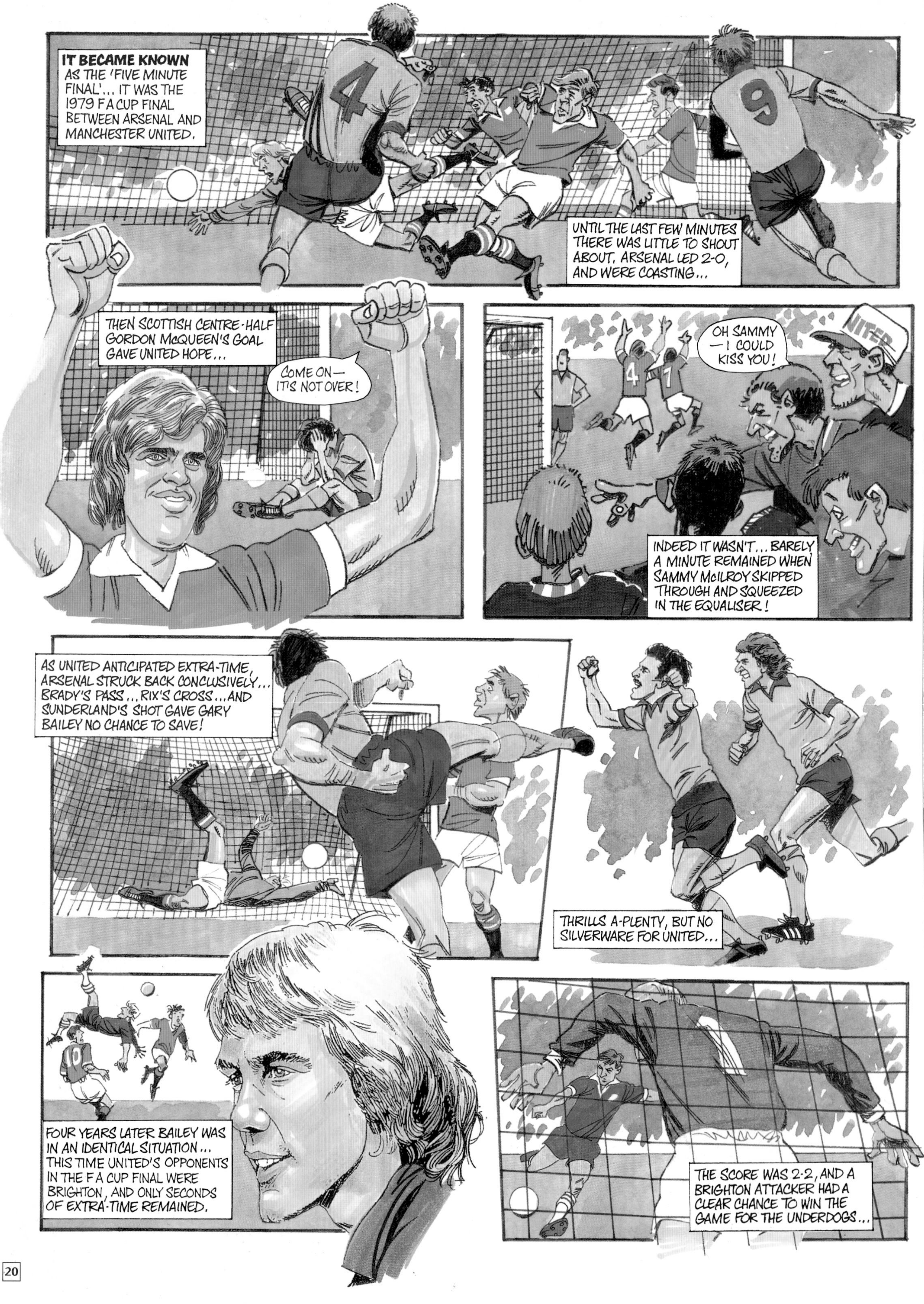
IT BECAME KNOWN AS THE 'FIVE MINUTE FINAL'... IT WAS THE 1979 F A CUP FINAL BETWEEN ARSENAL AND MANCHESTER UNITED.
UNTIL THE LAST FEW MINUTES THERE WAS LITTLE TO SHOUT ABOUT. ARSENAL LED 2-0, AND WERE COASTING...
THEN SCOTTISH CENTRE-HALF GORDON McQUEEN'S GOAL GAVE UNITED HOPE...
COME ON— IT'S NOT OVER!
OH SAMMY —I COULD KISS YOU!
INDEED IT WASN'T... BARELY A MINUTE REMAINED WHEN SAMMY McILROY SKIPPED THROUGH AND SQUEEZED IN THE EQUALISER!
AS UNITED ANTICIPATED EXTRA-TIME, ARSENAL STRUCK BACK CONCLUSIVELY... BRADY'S PASS... RIX'S CROSS... AND SUNDERLAND'S SHOT GAVE GARY BAILEY NO CHANCE TO SAVE!
THRILLS A-PLENTY, BUT NO SILVERWARE FOR UNITED...
FOUR YEARS LATER BAILEY WAS IN AN IDENTICAL SITUATION... THIS TIME UNITED'S OPPONENTS IN THE F A CUP FINAL WERE BRIGHTON, AND ONLY SECONDS OF EXTRA-TIME REMAINED.
THE SCORE WAS 2-2, AND A BRIGHTON ATTACKER HAD A CLEAR CHANCE TO WIN THE GAME FOR THE UNDERDOGS...

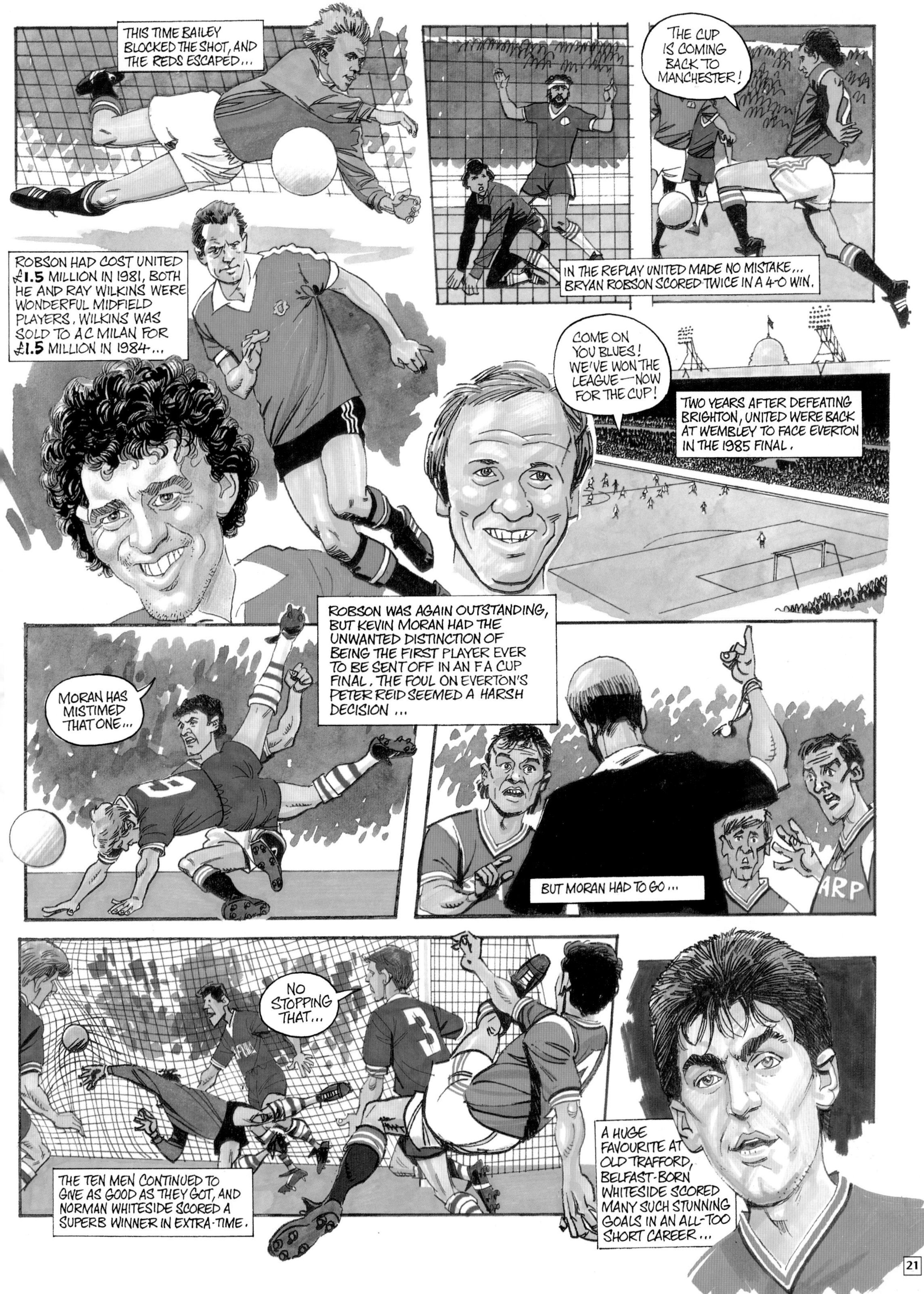

THIS TIME BAILEY BLOCKED THE SHOT, AND THE REDS ESCAPED...
THE CUP IS COMING BACK TO MANCHESTER!
IN THE REPLAY UNITED MADE NO MISTAKE... BRYAN ROBSON SCORED TWICE IN A 4-0 WIN.
ROBSON HAD COST UNITED £1.5 MILLION IN 1981, BOTH HE AND RAY WILKINS WERE WONDERFUL MIDFIELD PLAYERS. WILKINS WAS SOLD TO AC MILAN FOR £1.5 MILLION IN 1984...
COME ON YOU BLUES! WE'VE WON THE LEAGUE — NOW FOR THE CUP!
TWO YEARS AFTER DEFEATING BRIGHTON, UNITED WERE BACK AT WEMBLEY TO FACE EVERTON IN THE 1985 FINAL.
ROBSON WAS AGAIN OUTSTANDING, BUT KEVIN MORAN HAD THE UNWANTED DISTINCTION OF BEING THE FIRST PLAYER EVER TO BE SENT OFF IN AN FA CUP FINAL. THE FOUL ON EVERTON'S PETER REID SEEMED A HARSH DECISION...
MORAN HAS MISTIMED THAT ONE...
BUT MORAN HAD TO GO...
NO STOPPING THAT...
THE TEN MEN CONTINUED TO GIVE AS GOOD AS THEY GOT, AND NORMAN WHITESIDE SCORED A SUPERB WINNER IN EXTRA-TIME.
A HUGE FAVOURITE AT OLD TRAFFORD, BELFAST-BORN WHITESIDE SCORED MANY SUCH STUNNING GOALS IN AN ALL-TOO SHORT CAREER...

TOMMY TAYLOR

BOBBY CHARLTON

ROGER BYRNE

DUNCAN
EDWARDS

MANCHE
UNIT
LEGE

MARTIN
BUCHAN

BRYAN
ROBSON

PETER
SCHMEICHEL

DENIS LAW

ALEX STEPNEY

GEORGE BEST

ER
-D
DS

MARK HUGHES

ERIC CANTONA

SHARP

RYAN GIGGS

DAVID BECKHAM

STEVE
BRUCE

ROY KEANE

vodafone

DESPITE THESE TWO FA CUP WINS, UNITED SEEMED NO CLOSER TO WINNING THEIR FIRST LEAGUE TITLE SINCE 1967.

REDS LOSE TOUCH WITH LEAGUE LEADERS

IN NOVEMBER 1986 MANAGER RON ATKINSON WAS DISMISSED, AND ALEX FERGUSON, WHO'D BEEN BOSS OF ABERDEEN, WAS PUT IN CHARGE AT OLD TRAFFORD...

MY AMBITION IS TO MAKE UNITED A CHAMPIONSHIP WINNING SIDE ONCE MORE...

ALEX FERGUSON'S FIRST BIG SIGNING WAS BRIAN McCLAIR, FROM CELTIC, FOR £850,000, AND IN HIS FIRST SEASON THE SCOT SCORED 31 LEAGUE AND CUP GOALS.

THE NEW BOSS HAS SPENT WELL...

SHARP

MARK HUGHES HAD SPENT TWO UNHAPPY SEASONS WITH BARCELONA, AND RETURNED TO OLD TRAFFORD IN 1988, TO THE DELIGHT OF THE FANS.

WELCOME BACK, SPARKY!

STEVE BRUCE WAS ALSO BOUGHT FROM NORWICH, AND PAUL INCE CAME FROM WEST HAM.

HUH?

ALEX FERGUSON'S FIRST SUCCESS CAME NOT IN THE LEAGUE, BUT ONCE AGAIN IN THE FA CUP...

GOAL!

A DING-DONG SEMI-FINAL WITH NEIGHBOURING OLDHAM ATHLETIC ENDED AT **3-3**, NEIL WEBB SCORING ONE OF THE GOALS,

WEBB WAS AN ATTACKING MIDFIELDER, WITH A KNACK OF SCORING GOALS AT VITAL TIMES. HE'D JOINED UNITED FROM FOREST FOR £1.5 MILLION...

THE SEMI-FINAL REPLAY WAS WON—A MARK ROBINS GOAL IN EXTRA-TIME SEEING OFF OLDHAM'S BRAVE RESISTANCE...

AT WEMBLEY, UNITED MET CRYSTAL PALACE, MANAGED BY FORMER UNITED PLAYER STEVE COPPELL...

UNITED WERE LEADING 2-1 WHEN COPPELL MADE A MASTERLY SUBSTITUTION...

ON YOU GO, IAN...

SOON...

HE'S SCORED! 2-2!

IN EXTRA-TIME...

WRIGHT HAS SCORED AGAIN!

3-2 TO PALACE!

PALACE WERE JUST SEVEN MINUTES AWAY FROM WINNING THE CUP WHEN MARK HUGHES STRUCK HIS SECOND OF THE MATCH... 3-3!

FOR THE REPLAY, UNITED REPLACED GOALKEEPER JIM LEIGHTON WITH LES SEALEY, WHO WAS ON LOAN FROM LUTON AT THE TIME.

THE CUP FINAL WAS ONLY HIS THIRD APPEARANCE FOR THE REDS— CERTAINLY A CASE OF BEING IN THE RIGHT PLACE AT THE RIGHT TIME!

WEBB SET UP THE ONLY GOAL FOR LEE MARTIN, AND ALEX FERGUSON'S TEAM HAD WON THE FA CUP...

25

IN NOVEMBER 1990 UNITED DESTROYED ARSENAL AT HIGHBURY IN THE FOOTBALL LEAGUE CUP— LEE SHARPE SCORED A BRILLIANT HAT-TRICK IN A MEMORABLE 6-2 VICTORY...

WHAT DO YOU SAY HIS NAME IS?

A YOUNG WELSH GENIUS RYAN GIGGS MADE HIS FIRST APPEARANCE FOR THE REDS IN MARCH 1991, AND A FEW WEEKS LATER HE SCORED HIS FIRST GOAL, THE WINNER AGAINST MANCHESTER CITY.

BACK IN EUROPE, UNITED PROGRESSED COMFORTABLY TO THE CUP WINNERS' CUP FINAL, BARCELONA WERE FORMIDABLE OPPOSITION IN ROTTERDAM... MARK HUGHES WAS IRRESISTABLE THAT EVENING, AND PUT UNITED AHEAD...

REMEMBER ME?

...THEN DOUBLED THE ADVANTAGE IN THE SECOND HALF, HE TOOK THE BALL AROUND 'KEEPER BUSQUETS...

...AND DROVE IN A TERRIFIC SHOT FROM A NARROW ANGLE.

TAKE THAT ONE OUT OF THE NET!

RONALD KOEMAN CURLED A FREE-KICK PAST SEALEY, BUT UNITED HELD ON TO WIN.

IT WAS THEIR FIRST EUROPEAN TRIUMPH SINCE 1968.

IN THE FINAL OF THE LEAGUE CUP SHEFFIELD WEDNESDAY BEAT THEM BY THE ONLY GOAL...

OUCH!

DENIS IRWIN, FROM OLDHAM, AND GARY PALLISTER, FROM MIDDLESBROUGH, HAD JOINED UNITED AND BECOME ESTABLISHED MEMBERS OF THE DEFENCE.

ALEX FERGUSON THEN BOUGHT TOP DANISH 'KEEPER PETER SCHMEICHEL FROM BRONDBY IN AUGUST 1991, FOR £500,000...

I THINK WE'VE MADE THE BARGAIN BUY OF THE CENTURY...

THIS GUY ISN'T HUMAN...

SO IT WAS TO PROVE... SCHMEICHEL MADE A WINNING DEBUT AGAINST NOTTS COUNTY AT OLD TRAFFORD—AND DIDN'T CONCEDE A GOAL UNTIL HIS FIFTH GAME!

BY CHRISTMAS UNITED HAD LOST ONLY ONCE, AT SHEFFIELD WEDNESDAY, AND SEEMED CERTAIN TO WIN THE LEAGUE...

BUT A DISAPPOINTING END TO THE SEASON, WITH A BAD DEFEAT AT LIVERPOOL, ALLOWED LEEDS UNITED TO SNEAK PAST THEM AND TAKE THE TITLE...

WHEN YOU NEED A WIN, THIS IS NOT THE BEST PLACE TO COME...

GORDON STRACHAN, A FORMER OLD TRAFFORD FAVOURITE, WAS THE INSPIRATION AT ELLAND ROAD.

TOP MAN

UNITED HAD TO BE CONTENT WITH WINNING THE LEAGUE CUP, BEATING NOTTINGHAM FOREST AT WEMBLEY WITH A SINGLE BRIAN McCLAIR GOAL...

WE'VE DONE IT!

WELL PLAYED, BRIAN!

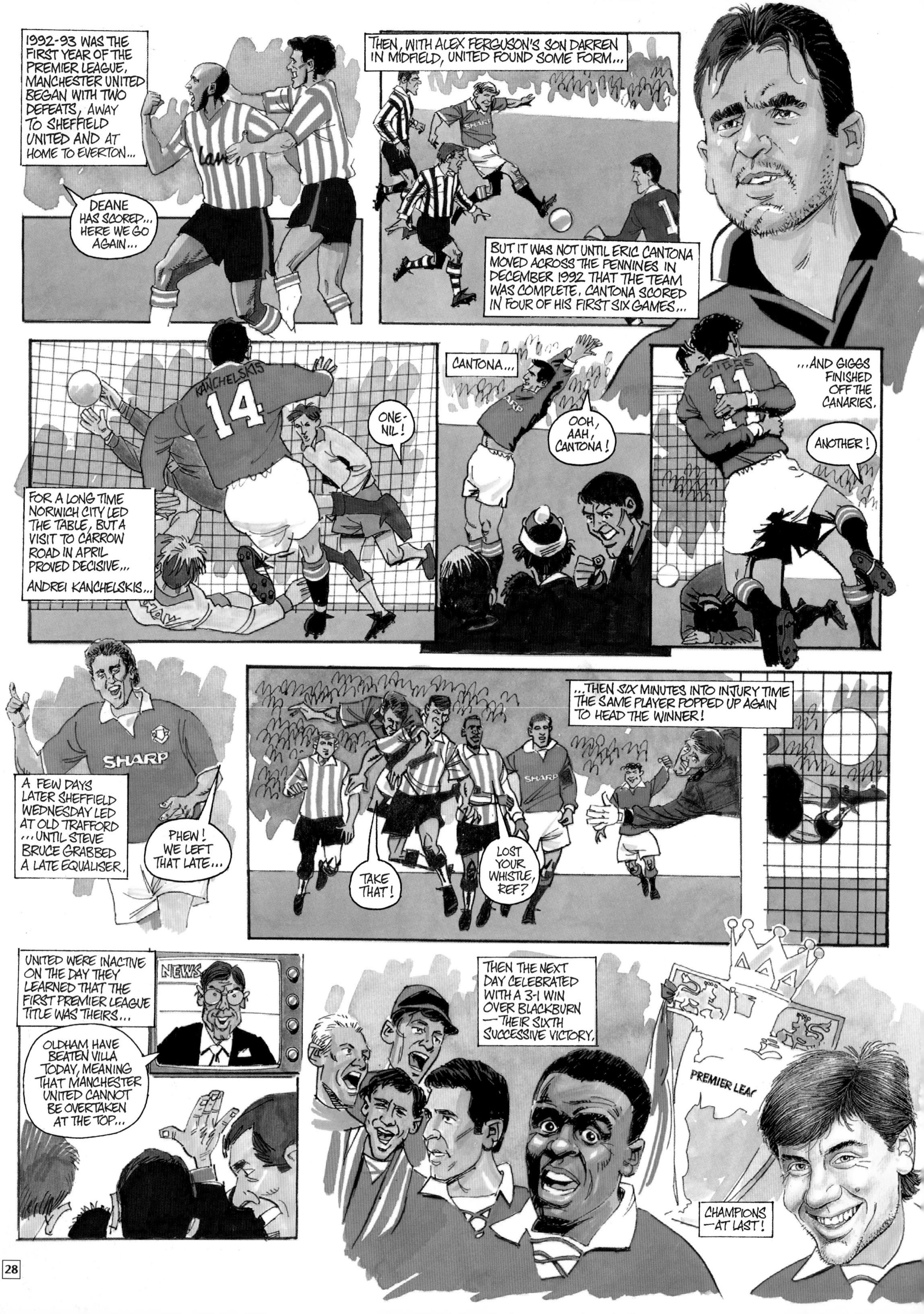
1992-93 WAS THE FIRST YEAR OF THE PREMIER LEAGUE. MANCHESTER UNITED BEGAN WITH TWO DEFEATS, AWAY TO SHEFFIELD UNITED AND AT HOME TO EVERTON...
DEANE HAS SCORED... HERE WE GO AGAIN...
THEN, WITH ALEX FERGUSON'S SON DARREN IN MIDFIELD, UNITED FOUND SOME FORM...
BUT IT WAS NOT UNTIL ERIC CANTONA MOVED ACROSS THE PENNINES IN DECEMBER 1992 THAT THE TEAM WAS COMPLETE. CANTONA SCORED IN FOUR OF HIS FIRST SIX GAMES...
FOR A LONG TIME NORWICH CITY LED THE TABLE, BUT A VISIT TO CARROW ROAD IN APRIL PROVED DECISIVE...
ANDREI KANCHELSKIS...
KANCHELSKIS 14
ONE-NIL!
CANTONA...
OOH, AAH, CANTONA!
...AND GIGGS FINISHED OFF THE CANARIES.
ANOTHER!
SHARP
A FEW DAYS LATER SHEFFIELD WEDNESDAY LED AT OLD TRAFFORD ...UNTIL STEVE BRUCE GRABBED A LATE EQUALISER.
PHEW! WE LEFT THAT LATE...
...THEN SIX MINUTES INTO INJURY TIME THE SAME PLAYER POPPED UP AGAIN TO HEAD THE WINNER!
TAKE THAT!
LOST YOUR WHISTLE, REF?
UNITED WERE INACTIVE ON THE DAY THEY LEARNED THAT THE FIRST PREMIER LEAGUE TITLE WAS THEIRS...
NEWS
OLDHAM HAVE BEATEN VILLA TODAY, MEANING THAT MANCHESTER UNITED CANNOT BE OVERTAKEN AT THE TOP...
THEN THE NEXT DAY CELEBRATED WITH A 3-1 WIN OVER BLACKBURN — THEIR SIXTH SUCCESSIVE VICTORY.
PREMIER LEA
CHAMPIONS — AT LAST!

IN 1993-94 UNITED WERE, IF ANYTHING, EVEN MORE IMPRESSIVE... ERIC CANTONA'S GOALS WERE ONCE AGAIN A DECISIVE FACTOR...

...AND WITH HUGHES, GIGGS AND KANCHELSKIS ALSO SCORING FREELY, THE REDS WERE SUPREME.

ROY KEANE WAS BOUGHT FROM FOREST FOR £3.75 MILLION, AND SCORED TWICE ON HIS HOME DEBUT.

HOW'S THAT FOR STARTERS?

CITY WERE BEATEN 3-2 AT MAINE ROAD IN A THRILLER.

BLACKBURN WERE THEIR MAIN RIVALS IN THE CHAMPIONSHIP RACE, ROVERS WERE A GOAL UP AT OLD TRAFFORD—UNTIL THE VERY LAST MINUTE...

COME ON, ROVERS—KEEP 'EM OUT!

THEN, WITH ALL THE UNITED PLAYERS—INCLUDING SCHMEICHEL—IN THE ROVERS BOX, INCE EQUALISED!

SCHMEICHEL?

WHAT'S HE DOING UP THERE?

IN JANUARY 1994 SIR MATT BUSBY DIED, AND THE CLUB MOURNED ITS MOST DISTINGUISHED SERVANT...

UNITED LED 3-0 AT ANFIELD...

BUT LIVERPOOL FOUGHT BACK TO LEVEL THE SCORES IN ANOTHER CLASSIC ENCOUNTER.

RUDDOCK HAS EQUALISED!

THE SEASON WAS STREWN WITH REMARKABLE GOALS... GIGGS SCORED AT QPR AFTER BEATING DEFENDER AFTER DEFENDER.

SOMEBODY STOP THAT MAN!

CANTONA GOT BOTH GOALS IN THE WIN OVER MANCHESTER CITY AT OLD TRAFFORD, AND SOON AFTERWARDS UNITED WERE CONFIRMED CHAMPIONS AGAIN...

WHILST SWEEPING ALL BEFORE THEM IN THE LEAGUE, THE REDS WERE ALSO MAKING A DETERMINED EFFORT TO WIN THE F A CUP...

BUT OLDHAM— AGAIN— WERE THEIR OPPONENTS IN THE SEMI-FINAL, AND UNTIL THE VERY LAST MINUTE THEY LED THEIR ILLUSTRIOUS NEIGHBOURS...

COME ON, BOYS...JUST ONE MORE MINUTE TO HOLD OUT...

SPARKY TO THE RESCUE!

THEN, RIGHT ON TIME, MARK HUGHES APPEARED IN THE PENALTY AREA TO THUNDER IN ONE OF HIS SPECIAL VOLLEYS...1-1!

UNITED WON THE REPLAY, AND MET CHELSEA ON A RAINY DAY AT WEMBLEY...

CHELSEA HAD BEATEN UNITED TWICE IN THE LEAGUE—EACH TIME WITH A GAVIN PEACOCK GOAL—AND FANCIED THEIR CHANCES...

HIM! AGAIN!

BUT WHEN PEACOCK'S FIRST HALF EFFORT BOUNCED OFF THE CROSSBAR, THEY KNEW IT WASN'T GOING TO BE THEIR DAY...

THAT'S CLOSE!

TWO CANTONA PENALTY-KICKS...

ANOTHER SCORCHER BY HUGHES...

AND A FOURTH FROM McCLAIR SAW UNITED COMFORTABLY HOME... TO A LEAGUE AND F A CUP DOUBLE.

IN 1995 UNITED WON NO TROPHIES, LOSING AT THE LAST HURDLE TO BLACKBURN IN THE CHAMPIONSHIP...

NEEDING TO WIN AT WEST HAM ON THE LAST DAY OF THE SEASON, UNITED SIMPLY COULD NOT GET THE WINNER,

THEN, SURPRISINGLY, THEY LOST TO A SINGLE EVERTON GOAL IN THE FA CUP FINAL...

THIS ISN'T SUPPOSED TO HAPPEN EITHER...

BUT ANDREW COLE HAD CAUSED A SENSATION WITH FIVE GOALS AGAINST IPSWICH, IN A 9-0 TROUNCING.

ENOUGH!

COLE HAD COST £6 MILLION FROM NEWCASTLE.

HUGHES, INCE AND KANCHELSKIS HAD ALL DEPARTED BY THE TIME THE 1995-96 SEASON BEGAN, AND CANTONA WAS SUSPENDED UNTIL OCTOBER...

YET ALEX FERGUSON RESISTED THE INCLINATION TO BUY NEW PLAYERS.

DAVID BECKHAM, NICKY BUTT, PAUL SCHOLES, AND THE BROTHERS PHILIP AND GARY NEVILLE WERE ALL IN THE TEAM FOR UNITED'S FIRST LEAGUE MATCH AT VILLA...

MY YOUNG PLAYERS ARE GOOD ENOUGH...

...AND THE YOUNG TEAM WERE SOUNDLY BEATEN! EVERYONE WAS QUICK TO GIVE THEIR OPINION OF UNITED'S CHANCES...

YOU DON'T WIN ANYTHING WITH KIDS...

WE'VE NO HOPE WITHOUT SOME NEW SIGNINGS...

AFTER THEIR OPENING DAY DEFEAT, FOLLOWED BY MUCH CRITICISM OF ALEX FERGUSON, HE KEPT FAITH IN HIS 'KIDS'... AND WON THE NEXT *FIVE* MATCHES

COME ON, UNITED!

WHO SCORED?

SCHMEICHEL, I THINK!

IT WASN'T WHAT THEY WANTED, BUT IT LEFT THEM FREE TO CONCENTRATE ON THE DOMESTIC COMPETITIONS...

GOAL!

THREE MORE POINTS!

DESPITE A GOAL FROM PETER SCHMEICHEL, UPFIELD FOR A SET PIECE, UNITED WENT OUT OF THE UEFA CUP AT THE FIRST HURDLE...

CANTONA RETURNED FROM SUSPENSION...

CAN-TONA! CAN-TONA!!!

...TO SCORE FROM A PENALTY KICK AGAINST LIVERPOOL IN A HARD-FOUGHT 2-2 DRAW.

IN JANUARY NEWCASTLE LED THE PREMIER LEAGUE BY *TEN* POINTS...

CATCH US IF YOU CAN...

...BUT THE REDS HAD SET OFF ON A RUN OF ALMOST UNINTERRUPTED SUCCESS, BOLTON, ON THEIR OWN GROUND, WERE HIT FOR *SIX*...

♫ CAN WE PLAY YOU EVERY WEEK..? ♪

THE FOLLOWING WEEK UNITED TRAVELLED TO NEWCASTLE, WHERE NO OTHER TEAM HAD WON SO FAR IN THE SEASON.

EARLY IN THE SECOND HALF...

THE FRENCHMAN HAS DONE IT AGAIN!

AFTER THAT, SCHMEICHEL WAS SUPERB, UNBEATEN AND UNBEATABLE.

ON THE LAST DAY OF THE SEASON MANCHESTER UNITED WENT TO BRYAN ROBSON'S MIDDLESBROUGH, KNOWING A WIN WOULD GIVE THEM THE TITLE AHEAD OF NEWCASTLE...

UNITED MUST DO THE BUSINESS THEMSELVES TODAY ...THEY CANNOT RELY ON NEWCASTLE LOSING...

IN HIS CAREER DAVID MAY HAD SCORED ONLY A COUPLE OF TIMES FOR UNITED, BUT...

GOAL!

MAY HAS DONE IT!

IT'S THERE!

THEN ANDREW COLE...

AND FINALLY...

3-0!

GIGGS!

CHAMPIONS!

ONCE AGAIN UNITED WERE CHAMPIONS, AND NEWCASTLE DENIED...

LIVERPOOL!

UNITED!

UNITED'S IRRESISTIBLE FORM HAD ALSO CARRIED THEM TO THE FA CUP FINAL AGAIN, BEATING MANCHESTER CITY AND CHELSEA ON THE WAY...

LIVERPOOL WERE EXPECTED TO STRETCH THEM TO THE LIMIT, BUT TYPICALLY CANTONA DELIVERED THE MATCH-WINNING STRIKE,

CAN-TONA!!!

HE'S DONE IT AGAIN!

MANCHESTER UNITED HAD DONE THE 'DOUBLE' ONCE MORE, NO OTHER ENGLISH CLUB HAD EVER ACHIEVED THIS TWICE...COULD IT GET ANY BETTER THAN THIS?

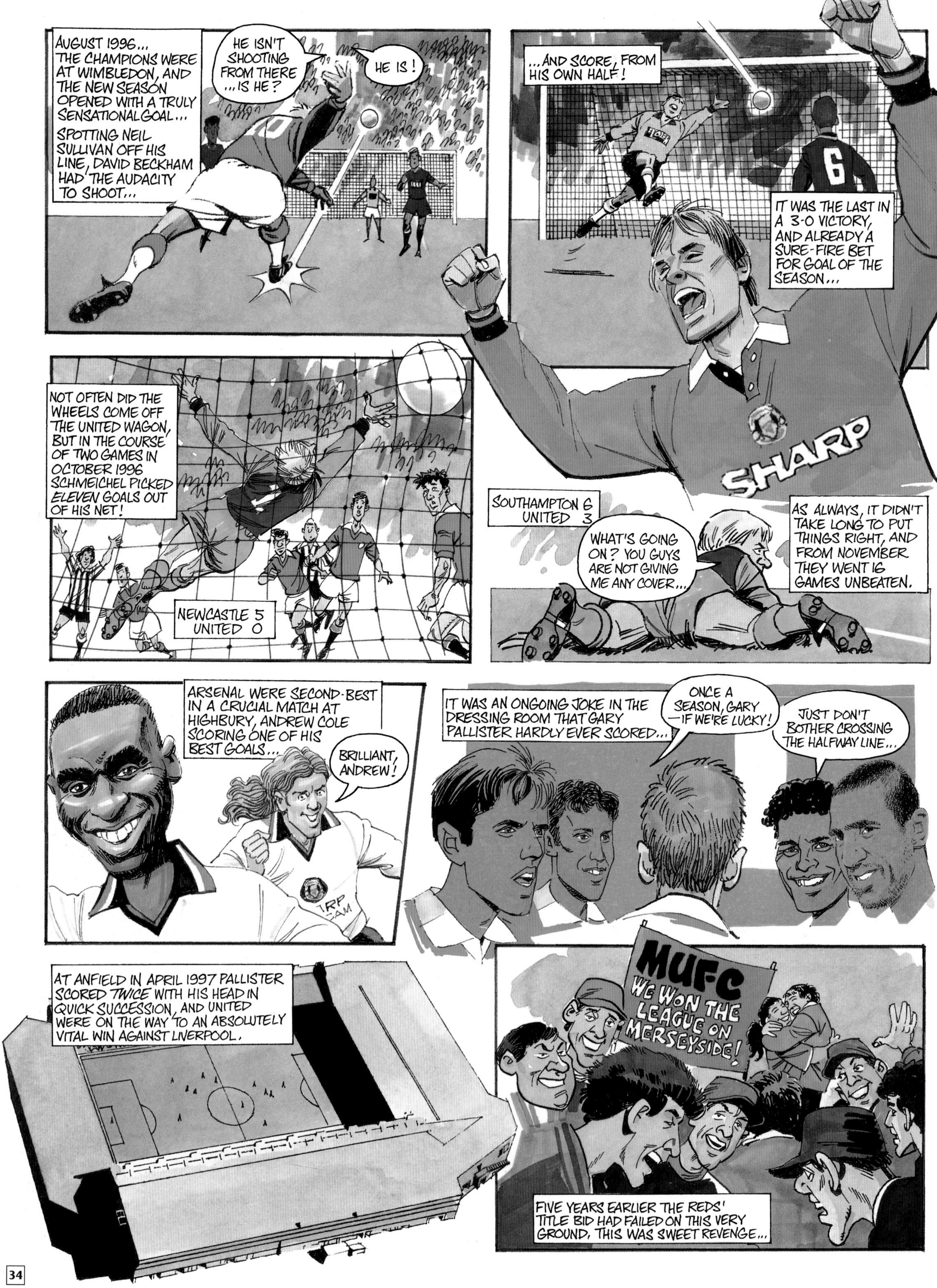
AUGUST 1996... THE CHAMPIONS WERE AT WIMBLEDON, AND THE NEW SEASON OPENED WITH A TRULY SENSATIONAL GOAL...
SPOTTING NEIL SULLIVAN OFF HIS LINE, DAVID BECKHAM HAD THE AUDACITY TO SHOOT...
HE ISN'T SHOOTING FROM THERE ...IS HE?
HE IS!
...AND SCORE, FROM HIS OWN HALF!
IT WAS THE LAST IN A 3-0 VICTORY, AND ALREADY A SURE-FIRE BET FOR GOAL OF THE SEASON...
SHARP
NOT OFTEN DID THE WHEELS COME OFF THE UNITED WAGON, BUT IN THE COURSE OF TWO GAMES IN OCTOBER 1996 SCHMEICHEL PICKED *ELEVEN* GOALS OUT OF HIS NET!
NEWCASTLE 5
UNITED 0
SOUTHAMPTON 6
UNITED 3
WHAT'S GOING ON? YOU GUYS ARE NOT GIVING ME ANY COVER...
AS ALWAYS, IT DIDN'T TAKE LONG TO PUT THINGS RIGHT, AND FROM NOVEMBER THEY WENT 16 GAMES UNBEATEN.
ARSENAL WERE SECOND-BEST IN A CRUCIAL MATCH AT HIGHBURY, ANDREW COLE SCORING ONE OF HIS BEST GOALS...
BRILLIANT, ANDREW!
IT WAS AN ONGOING JOKE IN THE DRESSING ROOM THAT GARY PALLISTER HARDLY EVER SCORED...
ONCE A SEASON, GARY —IF WE'RE LUCKY!
JUST DON'T BOTHER CROSSING THE HALFWAY LINE...
AT ANFIELD IN APRIL 1997 PALLISTER SCORED *TWICE* WITH HIS HEAD IN QUICK SUCCESSION, AND UNITED WERE ON THE WAY TO AN ABSOLUTELY VITAL WIN AGAINST LIVERPOOL.
MUFC
WE WON THE LEAGUE ON MERSEYSIDE!
FIVE YEARS EARLIER THE REDS' TITLE BID HAD FAILED ON THIS VERY GROUND. THIS WAS SWEET REVENGE...

IT WAS DOWNHILL ALL THE WAY AFTER THAT... AFTER THE FINAL HOME GAME, A 2-0 WIN OVER WEST HAM...

CHAMPIONS!

AGAIN!

...ERIC CANTONA HELD UP THE PREMIER LEAGUE TROPHY. IT WAS A FAMILIAR SCENE, BUT UNITED FANS WOULD NOT SEE CANTONA DO IT ANY MORE. HE HAD ALREADY ANNOUNCED HIS INTENTION TO CALL IT A DAY...

AU REVOIR, ERIC!

BON CHANCE!

THE ONLY DISAPPOINTMENT IN ANOTHER EXCELLENT SEASON WAS TO LOSE TO BORUSSIA DORTMUND IN THE SEMI-FINAL OF THE EUROPEAN CUP. 53,000 FANS SHOUTED AND SCREAMED FOR A GOAL, BUT NONE CAME...

HE MUST SCORE THIS TIME...

NOOOO...

1997-98... BY NOW THOSE FANS HAD GROWN USED TO SUCCESS, AND ANYTHING LESS THAN FIRST PLACE WAS A SHOCK TO THE SYSTEM...

TEDDY SHERINGHAM HAD WON NOTHING IN A WONDERFUL CAREER WITH SPURS, AND JUMPED AT THE CHANCE TO JOIN UNITED, WHO WOULDN'T? SOON HE WAS BANGING IN THE GOALS REGULARLY...

UNITED COULD HAVE SUCCESSFULLY DEFENDED THEIR TITLE, BUT...

WE HAVE TO BEAT ARSENAL TODAY...

IT'S EITHER US OR THEM FOR THE TITLE...

AGAINST ARSENAL, AT OLD TRAFFORD IN MARCH, THEY WERE OUTWITTED BY DUTCH MIDFIELDER MARC OVERMARS...

UNITED 0 ARSENAL 1

YOU WEREN'T MARKING HIM!

...AND THE TITLE WAS ON ITS WAY OUT OF OLD TRAFFORD.

IT'S A GOAL FOR THE FRENCH CHAMPIONS...

IN THE EUROPEAN CUP, DEFEAT BY MONACO IN THE QUARTER-FINALS LEFT UNITED, FOR ONCE, STARING AT AN EMPTY TROPHY CABINET...

REDS RULE COMES TO AN END

AUGUST 1998...
IN WHAT WAS TO BECOME UNITED'S GREATEST-EVER SEASON, THEY MADE A VERY HESITANT START. THEIR OPENING LEAGUE MATCH WAS AGAINST LEICESTER CITY AT OLD TRAFFORD...

OH, NO... THAT PUTS US TWO DOWN!

IT TOOK A SPECIAL DAVID BECKHAM FREE-KICK, DEEP INTO INJURY TIME, TO RESCUE A POINT...

2-2! WE GOT OUT OF JAIL...

BECKHAM HAD BEEN WIDELY BLAMED FOR ENGLAND'S WORLD CUP EXIT AT THE HANDS OF ARGENTINA A FEW WEEKS EARLIER, AND OPPOSING FANS WERE SLOW TO FORGIVE HIM...

UNITED HAD STRENGTHENED THEIR SQUAD DURING THE CLOSE SEASON. DUTCHMAN JAAP STAM, AFTER AN INDIFFERENT START, SOON BECAME A TOWER OF STRENGTH AT THE CENTRE OF THE DEFENCE...

DWIGHT YORKE, A £12 MILLION BUY FROM ASTON VILLA, SCORED ON HIS HOME DEBUT AGAINST CHARLTON...

BUT ARSENAL, THE REIGNING CHAMPIONS, THUMPED UNITED 3-0 AT HIGHBURY...

ARSENAL!

CHAMPIONS!

...AND A BAD HOME DEFEAT BY MIDDLESBROUGH HAD THE FANS FEARING THE WORST.

HAPPY CHRISTMAS, BRYAN ROBSON... WE CERTAINLY GIFT-WRAPPED ALL THREE POINTS TODAY!

BUT AFTER CHRISTMAS THE REDS EMBARKED ON A LONG, UNBEATEN RUN... LEICESTER WERE HIT FOR SIX ON THEIR OWN GROUND...

EVEN STAM HAS JOINED IN THE SCORING!

FOREST WERE ON THE RECEIVING END OF AN EVEN HEAVIER HOME DEFEAT, WITH NOT LONG LEFT FOR PLAY, UNITED WERE 4-1 AHEAD... AND ALEX FERGUSON DECIDED TO BRING OFF DWIGHT YORKE...

ON YOU GO, OLE... ENJOY YOURSELF!

IN THE REMAINING TEN MINUTES OLE GUNNAR SOLSKJAER ENJOYED HIMSELF SO MUCH THAT HE HELPED HIMSELF TO FOUR GOALS!

FOREST 1 UNITED 8!

AT THE END OF APRIL, ARSENAL STILL LED THE PREMIER LEAGUE...

WE'RE NOT GOING TO LET GO OF THIS TITLE WITHOUT A FIGHT...

OLD TRAFFORD MANCHESTER

WHEN THE VERY LAST MATCHES KICKED OFF, UNITED LED ARSENAL BY A SINGLE POINT, WHILE VILLA WERE AT HIGHBURY, SPURS WERE THE VISITORS TO OLD TRAFFORD...

IF THE FAITHFUL WERE READY FOR A CELEBRATION, LES FERDINAND SEEMED LIKE THE PARTY-POOPER... 1-0 TO SPURS!

NOOOO... WRONG NET!

EVEN WHEN BECKHAM EQUALISED...

...AND COLE PUT UNITED AHEAD...

SHARP

THE FANS STILL COULD NOT RELAX...

WHAT A TEAM!

ARSENAL ARE WINNING...

AT LAST THE FINAL WHISTLE SIGNALLED ANOTHER CHAMPIONSHIP SECURED...

SHARP

PREMIER

37

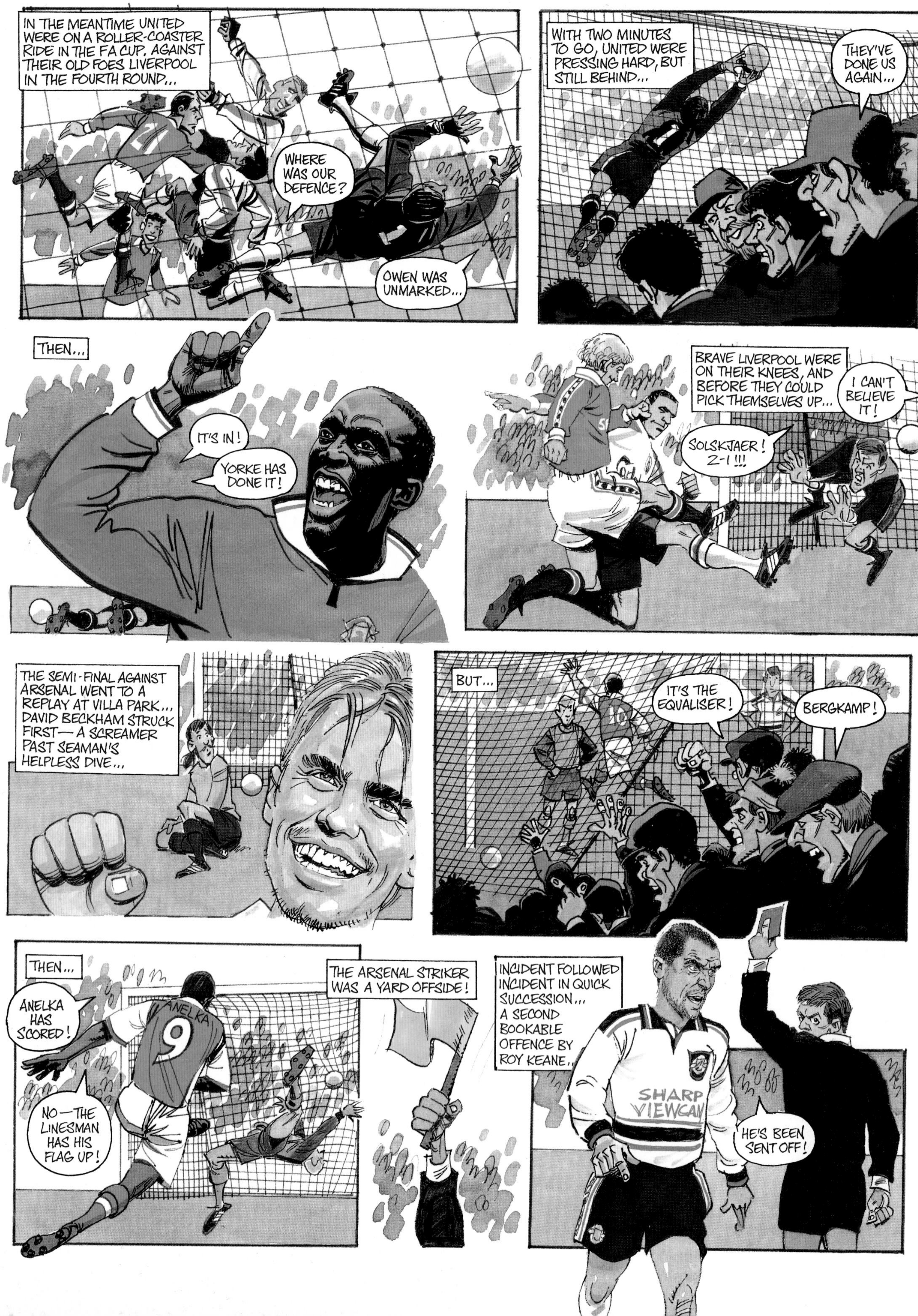
IN THE MEANTIME UNITED WERE ON A ROLLER-COASTER RIDE IN THE FA CUP, AGAINST THEIR OLD FOES LIVERPOOL IN THE FOURTH ROUND...
WHERE WAS OUR DEFENCE?
OWEN WAS UNMARKED...
WITH TWO MINUTES TO GO, UNITED WERE PRESSING HARD, BUT STILL BEHIND...
THEY'VE DONE US AGAIN...
THEN...
IT'S IN!
YORKE HAS DONE IT!
BRAVE LIVERPOOL WERE ON THEIR KNEES, AND BEFORE THEY COULD PICK THEMSELVES UP...
I CAN'T BELIEVE IT!
SOLSKJAER! 2-1 !!!
THE SEMI-FINAL AGAINST ARSENAL WENT TO A REPLAY AT VILLA PARK... DAVID BECKHAM STRUCK FIRST— A SCREAMER PAST SEAMAN'S HELPLESS DIVE...
BUT...
IT'S THE EQUALISER!
BERGKAMP!
THEN...
ANELKA HAS SCORED!
NO—THE LINESMAN HAS HIS FLAG UP!
THE ARSENAL STRIKER WAS A YARD OFFSIDE!
INCIDENT FOLLOWED INCIDENT IN QUICK SUCCESSION... A SECOND BOOKABLE OFFENCE BY ROY KEANE...
SHARP VIEWCAM
HE'S BEEN SENT OFF!

AGAINST TEN MEN, ARSENAL WERE NOW CLEAR FAVOURITES. A FLOWING MOVE... AND RAY PARLOUR WAS BROUGHT DOWN IN THE BOX...

PENALTY!

BERGKAMP COULD WIN THE MATCH, BUT...

SCHMEICHEL HAS SAVED IT!

WE ARE STILL IN WITH A CHANCE!

IN THE SECOND PERIOD OF EXTRA-TIME, RYAN GIGGS TOOK OVER, RACING FROM HIS OWN HALF, GIGGS LEFT A TRAIL OF ARSENAL DEFENDERS IN HIS WAKE...

SOMEBODY STOP HIM!

... BEFORE SMASHING THE BALL PAST SEAMAN!

ABSOLUTE MAGIC!

IT WAS ONE OF THE VERY GREATEST OF FA CUP GOALS...

ARSENAL 1 UNITED 2

MAY 1999... THE FA CUP FINAL AT WEMBLEY... MANCHESTER UNITED V NEWCASTLE THERE WAS AN EARLY BLOW FOR THE REDS AS SKIPPER ROY KEANE WENT DOWN...

SORRY... I CAN'T CONTINUE...

RIGHT, TEDDY— ON YOU GO!

SHERINGHAM HAD BEEN ON THE FIELD BARELY A MINUTE WHEN HE DROVE IN THE FIRST GOAL!

PAUL SCHOLES HIT THE SECOND, AND NEWCASTLE HAD NO ANSWER...

IT WAS UNITED'S TENTH FA CUP TRIUMPH, AND THEIR THIRD CUP AND LEAGUE DOUBLE!

TWO OUT OF THREE...

AS THE DRAW WAS MADE FOR THE EUROPEAN CHAMPIONS LEAGUE, IT WAS CALLED THE 'GROUP OF DEATH'...

MANCHESTER UNITED WILL PLAY IN THE SAME GROUP AS...BARCELONA ...AND BAYERN MUNICH!

THERE WAS AN INDICATION OF HOW HARD IT WOULD BE IN THE OPENING MATCH AGAINST BARCELONA. UNITED LED TWICE...

...BUT HAD TO SETTLE FOR A 3-3 DRAW.

IN THE RETURN MATCH IN THE NOU CAMP STADIUM, BARCELONA AGAIN FOUGHT BACK TO DRAW 3-3. AFTER ALL THE GROUP GAMES WERE COMPLETED, UNITED WENT THROUGH...BUT BARCELONA WENT OUT...

IN THEIR QUARTER-FINAL WITH INTER MILAN IT NEEDED A LATE GOAL BY PAUL SCHOLES IN THE SECOND LEG, IN THE SAN SIRO STADIUM, TO ENSURE UNITED'S PROGRESS...

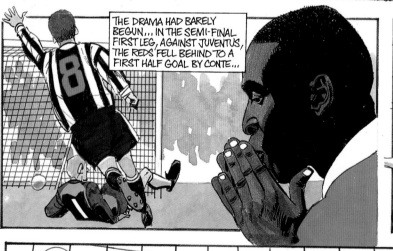

THE DRAMA HAD BARELY BEGUN... IN THE SEMI-FINAL FIRST LEG, AGAINST JUVENTUS, THE 'REDS' FELL BEHIND TO A FIRST HALF GOAL BY CONTE...

DESPITE CONSTANT HOME PRESSURE THE SCORE WAS UNCHANGED AS THE GAME MOVED INTO INJURY TIME, THEN...

RYAN GIGGS!

GOAL!

AT LAST! 1-1!!!

JUVENTUS AGAIN SCORED EARLY IN THE SECOND LEG IN ITALY—NOT ONCE, BUT TWICE!

WE'VE HAD IT THIS TIME...

IT'S A LONG WAY HOME TO MANCHESTER...

BUT THE TRIP HOME WAS TO BE AN ENJOYABLE ONE, AS FIRST KEANE...

...THEN YORKE

...AND FINALLY COLE ENDED JUVE'S HOPES

JUVENTUS 2
MANCHESTER UNITED 3!

MAY 1999...
THE EUROPEAN CUP FINAL—UNITED V BAYERN MUNICH IN BARCELONA...

TREBLE CHANCE REDS

I DON'T WANT TO SEEM GREEDY, BUT...

WOULDN'T IT BE GREAT?

IN FIVE MINUTES BAYERN HAD THE LEAD!

SHUCKS! WHY DO WE ALWAYS GIVE THE OPPOSITION A GOAL START?

FOR THE REST OF THE GAME UNITED STROVE FOR AN EQUALISER WHICH LOOKED LIKE WOULD NEVER COME...

AT THE OTHER END, BAYERN HAD CHANCES TO PUT THE GAME BEYOND UNITED'S REACH...

SCHMEICHEL!

OFF THE POST...

AND THE CROSSBAR!

LUCK IS CERTAINLY ON OUR SIDE...

THEN, THE MOST DRAMATIC TWO MINUTES IN THE CLUB'S HISTORY... THE GAME HAD GONE INTO ADDED TIME WHEN SHERINGHAM TURNED IN THE EQUALISER!

PICK THAT ONE OUT!

THERE WAS STILL TIME FOR ONE MORE RAID ON THE BAYERN GOAL... STUNNED, THE GERMAN TEAM'S DEFENCE WAS STATIC AS SOLSKJAER, FROM A YARD OUT, TOUCHED IN BECKHAM'S CORNER!

OHHH YESSS!!!

A WONDERFUL NIGHT, AND NOW THE CELEBRATIONS COULD REALLY BEGIN...

41

TEDDY SHERINGHAM MUST HAVE THOUGHT ALL HIS BIRTHDAYS HAD COME AT ONCE—THREE TROPHIES. AFTER ALL THOSE BARREN YEARS, HE WAS TO WIN MORE BEFORE IN 2001 RETURNING TO SPURS...

SCHMEICHEL HAD PLAYED HIS LAST MATCH FOR UNITED IN BARCELONA, AND SIR ALEX FERGUSON HAD TO REPLACE THE IRREPLACEABLE.

MARK BOSNICH WAS SIGNED, BUT WAS INJURED IN ONLY HIS THIRD START...

HE'LL BE OUT FOR WEEKS, BOSS...

WE NEED TO LOOK FOR ANOTHER GOALIE...

MASSIMO TAIBI CAME WITH A GOOD REPUTATION AS A GOALKEEPER, BUT DIDN'T HAVE MUCH LUCK. CHELSEA STUCK FIVE PAST HIM...

HOW MANY THAT? I LOSE COUNT...

UNITED WERE STILL FLYING HIGH, HOWEVER, WITH ANDREW COLE SCORING FOUR TIMES AGAINST HIS FORMER CLUB, NEWCASTLE...

WE'RE NOT STILL FRIENDS, THEN?

SIR ALEX WAS UNSHAKEN IN HIS RESOLVE...

GOALKEEPER CRAIG FORREST HAD BEEN IN THE IPSWICH TEAM BEATEN 9-0 AT OLD TRAFFORD IN 1995.

THE FANS WATCHED IN GLEEFUL ANTICIPATION AS HE TROTTED OUT TO PLAY FOR WEST HAM...

ONLY SEVEN THIS TIME, CRAIG—IT'S NOT TOO BAD...

OUR PRIORITY IS ALWAYS TO WIN THE LEAGUE...

COLE AND YORKE WERE ONCE AGAIN THE MOST EFFECTIVE DOUBLE ACT IN THE PREMIER LEAGUE —39 GOALS BETWEEN THEM...

NONE OF UNITED'S GOALS WERE HIS FAULT...

UNITED'S BIGGEST DISAPPOINTMENT WAS THEIR FAILURE TO RETAIN THE EUROPEAN CUP— LOSING IN THE QUARTER-FINALS TO OLD RIVALS REAL MADRID...

IT'S IN THE NET...

NO MORE EUROPEAN TRAVELS THIS YEAR...

UNITED!

THEY BOUNCED BACK A FEW DAYS LATER WITH A 3-1 WIN AT SOUTHAMPTON, TO CLINCH ANOTHER PREMIER LEAGUE TITLE WITH FOUR MATCHES STILL TO PLAY...

GET IN THERE...

CHAMPIONS! AGAIN!

So, CHAMPIONS AGAIN... IN 2000-2001 COULD ARSENAL, LEEDS, OR ANY OTHER BIG PREMIER LEAGUE SIDE STOP THE UNITED WAGON ROLLING ON..?

BEFORE THE SEASON BEGAN UNITED SORTED OUT THEIR GOALKEEPING PROBLEMS BY SIGNING FABIEN BARTHEZ, FRANCE'S FIRST CHOICE CUSTODIAN,

WOW! WHAT A SAVE...

HE'S A BIT SPECIAL!

HAVE WE STARTED, THEN?

THE MUCH-AWAITED DERBY WITH MANCHESTER CITY WAS SETTLED BY A DAVID BECKHAM GOAL IN THE SECOND MINUTE...

...ONE OF EIGHT SUCCESSIVE VICTORIES WHICH TOOK UNITED TO A VERY FAMILIAR TOP SPOT.

TOP OF THE LEAGUE AGAIN...

THE KEY MATCH AGAINST ARSENAL WAS OVER AS A CONTEST IN 22 MINUTES— THE TIME IT TOOK FOR DWIGHT YORKE TO COMPLETE HIS HAT-TRICK.

WHY DO YOU LET HIM GET SO NEAR..?

FINAL SCORE, 6-1...

APRIL 2001... ARSENAL'S HOME MATCH WITH MIDDLESBROUGH HAD AN EARLY KICK-OFF, AND UNITED WERE ABLE TO WATCH THEIR NEAREST RIVALS PLAY...
'BORO SCORED THREE WITHOUT REPLY...

...SO EVEN BEFORE THEY KICKED OFF AGAINST COVENTRY, MANCHESTER UNITED KNEW THAT THE TITLE WAS RETAINED. THEY CELEBRATED WITH A 4-2 VICTORY...

IN THE NINE SEASONS SINCE THE PREMIER LEAGUE BEGAN, UNITED HAD WON IT SEVEN TIMES,

THE TITLE IS OURS...

NOW LET'S GO OUT AND PLAY LIKE CHAMPIONS!

I COULD GET USED TO THIS...

43

2001-2002 WILL BE MY LAST SEASON AS MANAGER OF MANCHESTER UNITED. THE CLUB SHOULD BEGIN TO LOOK FOR MY SUCCESSOR...

THANKFULLY SIR ALEX FERGUSON WAS LATER PREVAILED UPON TO CHANGE HIS MIND. UNITED WENT INTO THE NEW SEASON WITH CONFIDENCE...

..., BOOSTED BY THE EXPENSIVE SIGNINGS OF JUAN SEBASTIAN VERON AND RUUD VAN NISTELROOY. ARGENTINEAN INTERNATIONAL VERON WAS A £28 MILLION SIGNING FROM LAZIO...

UNITED HAD TRIED TO GET VAN NISTELROOY A YEAR EARLIER, BUT THE DEAL HAD BEEN POSTPONED BECAUSE OF A HORRIFIC INJURY...

WELCOME TO THE PREMIER LEAGUE, EDWIN!

NOW FULLY RECOVERED, HE ANNOUNCED HIS ARRIVAL WITH TWO GOALS PAST HIS OWN COUNTRY'S GOALIE, EDWIN VAN DER SAR. UNITED BEAT FULHAM 3-2...

JAAP STAM HAD DEPARTED AND BEEN REPLACED BY LAURENT BLANC, FRANCE'S WORLD CUP WINNING DEFENDER...

UNITED WERE STILL THE TEAM EVERYONE WANTED TO BEAT..., AND EVEN WHEN YOU THOUGHT THEY WERE BEATEN, THEY WEREN'T...

IN SEPTEMBER 2001 UNITED VISITED SPURS, WHO HAD JUST SIGNED DEAN RICHARDS FROM SOUTHAMPTON. THE NEWCOMER SOON HAD THE FANS ON HIS SIDE...

GOAL!

WHO SCORED?

RICHARDS!

IT GOT WORSE FOR UNITED, LES FERDINAND SCORED A SECOND, THEN...

ZIEGE THIS TIME!

IT'S ONE-WAY TRAFFIC!

HALF-TIME, 3-0!

I WOULD LOVE TO BE A FLY ON THE WALL OF UNITED'S DRESSING-ROOM...

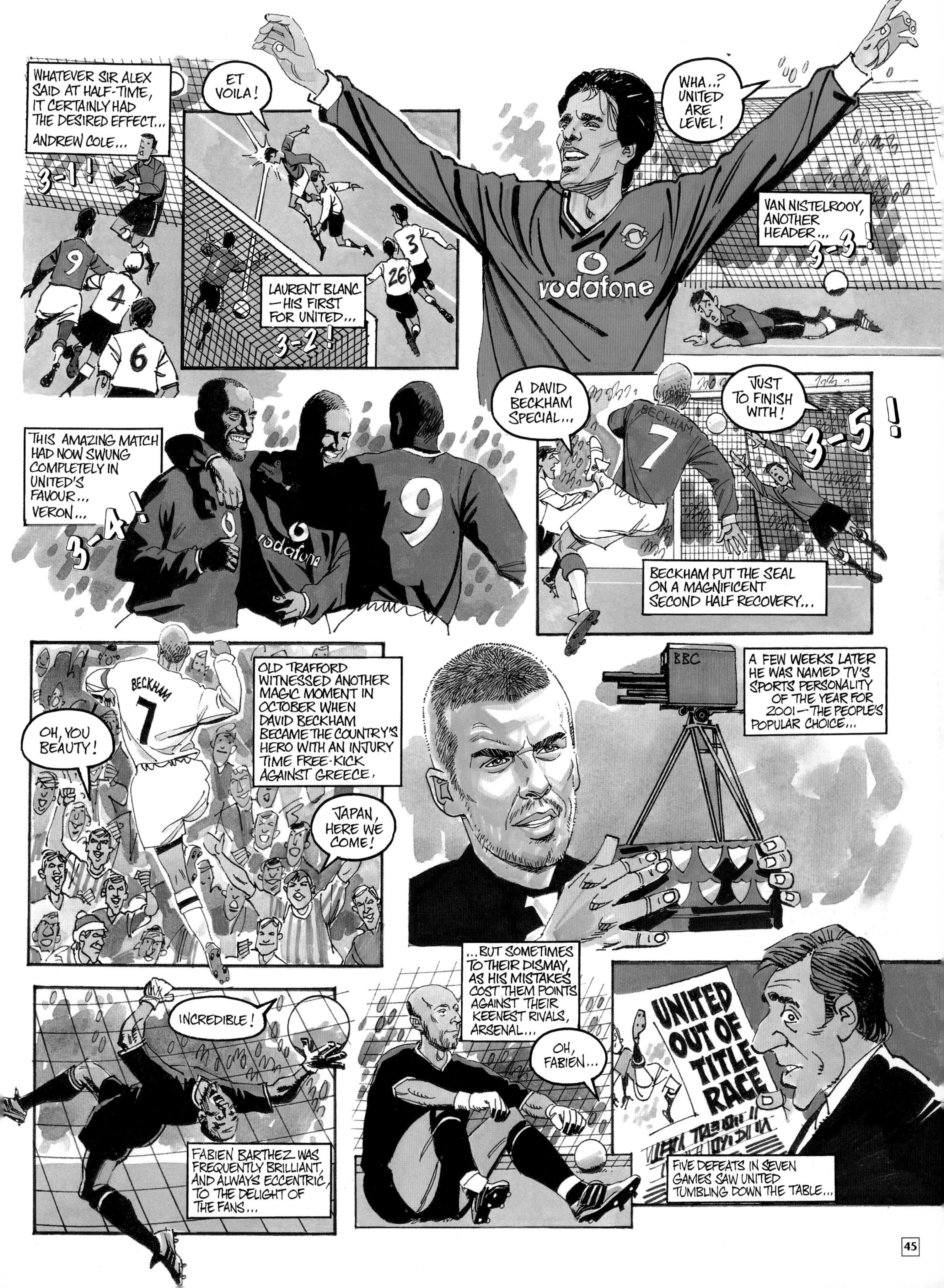
WHATEVER SIR ALEX SAID AT HALF-TIME, IT CERTAINLY HAD THE DESIRED EFFECT... ANDREW COLE...
3-1!
ET VOILA!
LAURENT BLANC — HIS FIRST FOR UNITED...
3-2!
WHA..? UNITED ARE LEVEL!
VAN NISTELROOY, ANOTHER HEADER...
3-3!
THIS AMAZING MATCH HAD NOW SWUNG COMPLETELY IN UNITED'S FAVOUR... VERON...
3-4!
A DAVID BECKHAM SPECIAL...
JUST TO FINISH WITH!
3-5!
BECKHAM PUT THE SEAL ON A MAGNIFICENT SECOND HALF RECOVERY...
OLD TRAFFORD WITNESSED ANOTHER MAGIC MOMENT IN OCTOBER WHEN DAVID BECKHAM BECAME THE COUNTRY'S HERO WITH AN INJURY TIME FREE-KICK AGAINST GREECE.
OH, YOU BEAUTY!
JAPAN, HERE WE COME!
A FEW WEEKS LATER HE WAS NAMED TV'S SPORTS PERSONALITY OF THE YEAR FOR 2001 — THE PEOPLE'S POPULAR CHOICE...
BBC
INCREDIBLE!
FABIEN BARTHEZ WAS FREQUENTLY BRILLIANT, AND ALWAYS ECCENTRIC, TO THE DELIGHT OF THE FANS...
...BUT SOMETIMES TO THEIR DISMAY, AS HIS MISTAKES COST THEM POINTS AGAINST THEIR KEENEST RIVALS, ARSENAL...
OH, FABIEN...
UNITED OUT OF TITLE RACE
FIVE DEFEATS IN SEVEN GAMES SAW UNITED TUMBLING DOWN THE TABLE...

NEVER MORE DANGEROUS THAN WHEN WRITTEN OFF, THE REDS WENT ON A RUN OF VICTORIES AS THEIR FORM RETURNED. GOALS FLOWED FREELY AGAIN — IF VAN NISTELROOY DIDN'T GET YOU, SOLSKJAER DID...

MY TURN TO SCORE...

THEY WERE STILL THE MOST EXCITING TEAM IN THE LAND...

I BELIEVE WE ARE AS GOOD AS AT ANY TIME SINCE I CAME HERE...

ALTHOUGH WEST HAM SCORED THREE TIMES AT UPTON PARK, UNITED BEAT THEM WITH A BRILLIANT ATTACKING DISPLAY, ILLUMINATED BY ANOTHER WONDERFUL GOAL BY BECKHAM.

ELLAND ROAD IN MARCH WAS THE SCENE OF A THRILLER ... AT THEIR MOST IRRESISTABLE, THE REDS RACED TO A 4-1 LEAD...

BUT AS LEEDS FOUGHT BACK SPIRITEDLY, IT WAS UNITED WHO WERE GLAD TO HEAR THE FINAL WHISTLE...

4-3... PHEW!

THE REDS GAVE THEIR FANS SOME MORE GOALS TO REMEMBER IN 2001-2002 — NONE BETTER THAN THE TERRIFIC STRIKE BY PAUL SCHOLES WHICH BEGAN THE DEMOLITION OF CHELSEA...

WHERE DID THAT COME FROM?

BUT ARSENAL HAD GAMES IN HAND, AND WERE ALSO PLAYING EXCITING FOOTBALL, UNITED TOOK IT TO THE LAST WEEK OF THE SEASON, THEN HAD TO CONCEDE THE LEAGUE TITLE.

MANCHESTER UNITED CONTINUED TO FLY THE FLAG IN EUROPE, PROGRESSING FURTHER THAN THE OTHER BRITISH TEAMS...
...BUT INJURIES TO KEY PLAYERS WERE FOLLOWED BY DEFEAT AT THE HANDS OF BAYER LEVERKUSEN IN THE EUROPEAN CHAMPIONS CUP.

MANCHESTER UNITED

FOR MORE UNITED GLORY, WATCH THIS SPACE!

THE TROPHY ROOM AT OLD TRAFFORD IS THE MOST IMPRESSIVE IN THE LAND. UNITED WON THE OLD FIRST DIVISION CHAMPIONSHIP **SEVEN** TIMES, AND HAVE BEEN PREMIER LEAGUE TITLE WINNERS IN **SEVEN** OF THE ELEVEN SEASONS IT HAS BEEN CONTESTED. THE CLUB HAS ALSO WON THE F.A. CUP **TEN** TIMES, AND THE EUROPEAN CUP **TWICE**.

THE DRESSING ROOMS ARE THE BEST, AS BEFITS SOME OF THE FINEST PLAYERS IN THE WORLD. 30 YEARS AGO UNITED HAD AS MANY AS **20** INTERNATIONALS ON THEIR PLAYING STAFF AT ONE TIME, AND THAT CONTINUES TODAY WITH PLAYERS FROM MANY COUNTRIES.

10,000 PIES ARE EATEN AT EVERY UNITED GAME AT OLD TRAFFORD....

DENNIS VIOLLET (LEFT) SCORED **32** LEAGUE GOALS IN 1959-60, STILL A CLUB RECORD. BOBBY CHARLTON MADE THE MOST APPEARANCES FOR UNITED, AND ALSO SCORED MOST GOALS—199!

WHEN FULL, THIS WONDERFUL STADIUM WILL HOLD OVER **68,000** SPECTATORS. FOR THAT THRILLING F.A. CUP TIE AGAINST LIVERPOOL IN 1999, A RECORD £850,000 WAS TAKEN IN GATE MONEY.

BATHS, INJURY TREATMENT ROOMS AND OTHER FACILITIES ARE EQUALLY EXCELLENT. LITTLE WONDER OLD TRAFFORD IS KNOWN AS THE THEATRE OF DREAMS. UNITED WERE UNBEATEN IN **29** CONSECUTIVE LEAGUE GAMES FROM DECEMBER 1998 UNTIL OCTOBER 1999....

THIS IS THE PRESS ROOM, WHERE MANAGERS AND PLAYERS GIVE THEIR AFTER-MATCH COMMENTS AND OPINIONS. EXPENSIVE NEW SIGNINGS ARE INTRODUCED TO THE MEDIA HERE....

First published in 2002

10 9 8 7 6 5 4 3 2 1

Manufactured and distributed by Manchester United Books
an imprint of Carlton Books Limited, 20 Mortimer Street, London W1T 3JW

A CIP catalogue record for this book is available from the British Library

ISBN 0 233 05074 4

Art & Script: Bob Bond
Project Editor: Martin Corteel
Project Art Director: Jim Lockwood
Production: Sarah Corteel

Printed in Italy